LIVING YOUR
LEADERSHIP

LIVING YOUR LEADERSHIP

GROW INTENTIONALLY, THRIVE WITH INTEGRITY, AND SERVE HUMBLY

CHRIS EWING, PhD

LIVING YOUR LEADERSHIP GROW INTENTIONALLY, THRIVE WITH INTEGRITY, AND SERVE HUMBLY

THE HOLY BIBLE, NEW INTERNATIONAL VERSION®, NIV® Copyright © 1973, 1978, 1984, 2011 by Biblica, Inc.® Used by permission. All rights reserved worldwide.

Scripture quotations from the Holy Bible, King James Version (Authorized Version). First published in 1611. Quoted from the KJV Classic Reference Bible.

iUniverse books may be ordered through booksellers or by contacting:

iUniverse
1663 Liberty Drive
Bloomington, IN 47403
www.iuniverse.com
1-800-Authors (1-800-288-4677)

ISBN: 978-1-5320-4001-6 (sc)
ISBN: 978-1-5320-4002-3 (e)

Library of Congress Control Number: 2018900557

Print information available on the last page.

iUniverse rev. date: 02/07/2018

CONTENTS

Foreword.. ix
Introduction.. xiii

LEADING YOURSELF

Grow Intentionally 1
Temet Nosce.. 10
Integrity and Mentorship... 22
Critical Reflection.. 31
Optimism and Gratitude 46
Leading with Humility 52
Application of Self-Leadership.. 64

LEADING OTHERS

Management versus Leadership.. 73
Respect and Human Dignity 83
Leading with Empathy 93
Live Authentically.. 101
Control and Autonomy 110
Leading Teams 122
Servant Leadership 132

DENOUEMENT

Pitfalls.. 149
Wrap-Up: Living Your Leadership.. 155
Acknowledgments.. 159

Abbreviations.. 161
References 163
Additional References and Recommended Reading...................... 175
About the Author 177

LIST OF FIGURES

Figure 1. Improving organizational leadership competency xx

Figure 2. The Living Your Leadership theoretical framework xxi

Figure 3. Self-talk loop 13

Figure 4. Emotional intelligence 15

Figure 5. Triadic reciprocal determinism 16

Figure 6. Modified Maslow's hierarchy of needs 18

Figure 7. Collins' Level 5 hierarchy 59

Figure 8. The humorless boss 61

Figure 9. A taxonomy of human motivation 67

Figure 10. The Eisenhower box 78

Figure 11. Pareto graph 80

Figure 12. Authority crushes autonomy 87

Figure 13. The circle of dialogical pedagogy 103

Figure 14. Locus of control continuum 113

Figure 15. Tuckman's stages of group formation 124

Figure 16. Yerkes-Dodson interpretation (replace *arousal* with *pressure*) ... 128

Figure 17. Balance in Living Your Leadership 154

FOREWORD

Colonel Marné Deranger, USAF, Retired

Perhaps you've heard the cliché "You manage resources but lead people." It comes up often in leadership training as reminder: do not treat people as resources. People aren't interchangeable cogs in the wheel, and as a leader, you will get better performance from them if you appreciate that fact (and them, for that matter—appreciate them). Your followers are people, complete with messy emotions, backstories, families, friends, hobbies, and lives outside of the workplace. Sometimes that spills over into the workplace, affecting their performance. Most of the time, it doesn't.

As a leader, there will be situations when you have to get your people to compartmentalize and push through—but you can't do that all the time. That must be for only special occasions. The rest of the time, you need to remember they are people. You don't have to hug them, hold hands, and sing each morning. It isn't day care. You just need to be aware. Always aware. In addition, you have to extend that awareness to yourself as a leader. You need to remember you are a person too and balance accordingly. Train accordingly. Give proper time, study, and effort into improving your leadership as a person. Not selfless. Not selfish. Just self-aware.

Chris Ewing always struck me as incredibly self-aware. He is a thoughtful person. Not thoughtful as in cards and flowers (though I'm sure that's true too) but in how he thinks about everything. While many might see how action A produces result B, and be content with repeating action A next time, Chris wants to know why. Chris wants to know if action A only produced result B given one situation, one individual, and one moment in time. Or can it be repeated? Chris wants to pick apart action A to see if it could produce even better results, given a tweak or two.

Chris is a leader who refuses to be satisfied by success. He dissects, he studies, and he thoughtfully ponders. He devotes significant time and energy to his own continuous improvement. Chris turned that drive for continuous improvement onto the question of leadership and found that even that wasn't sufficient. Leadership is easy to talk about, harder to do, and even more difficult to write about. Luckily, Chris doesn't shy away from a challenge. It wasn't enough for him to study leadership; he wanted to share what he learned, like the true servant leader he is. Thus, *Living Your Leadership* was born.

You might wonder if this book is for you, though. So I ask this question: Are you satisfied with your leadership performance? If you say yes, stop reading now. (Of course, you are terribly wrong, but we won't talk about that here.) However, if you feel you could improve, if you want to do better, if you strive to be a good example of leadership, if you seek greater leadership challenges, then read on. In the following pages, Dr. Ewing will lead you through his theory-to-practice approach, demonstrating how to use the most credible scientific research to your best advantage.

Chris starts, as one should, with self-leadership. As you will read later in this book, "Authentic servant leadership relies on the understanding that a leader is primarily concerned not with themselves but with others." An effective leader cannot be only outwardly focused. Just as you should affix your own oxygen mask before assisting others, leaders must look inward before attempting to lead others. We must understand our authentic selves; develop self-regulatory behaviors; and learn about integrity, self-reflection, and humility before we can apply the other leadership lessons.

The second section of the book moves the focus outward. Dr. Ewing discusses the importance of empathy, authenticity, autonomy, and servant leadership using positive and negative examples from his career. Most importantly, he addresses a point that many overlook: leadership is essentially a relationship, and relationships require trust. From the chapter on team leadership: "Transparency and integrity are key components of establishing trust in an organization because they are fundamental aspects of relationship building." If your team trusts you as a leader, you can overcome any obstacle. However, as a leader, you must trust yourself first. The critical self-reflection in the following pages will help you do that.

In his own self-reflection, Chris saw the chance I took when I hired him. But really, don't we take chances in leadership positions every day? We take chances because we work with people, and people are unique. This individuality can be a weakness or strength to your organization, depending on how you perceive it and yourself. Hearty self-reflection hones your instincts as a leader. Because I trusted my instincts and the insights of peers I trusted, our organization gained a valuable, intelligent employee. One who questioned and studied and was never satisfied with the status quo. A leader who has continued to grow and live the lessons he spells out in this book: he is the quintessential servant leader.

Enjoy.

INTRODUCTION

LIVING YOUR LEADERSHIP®

The very fact that leadership is an art should discourage your becoming a mechanical leader. Leadership does not provide formulas, rules, or methods which will fit every situation. Leadership is an intangible quality which cannot be seen, felt, or measured except through its results. Moreover, you cannot predict the results with mathematical accuracy. If you have skill as a leader, however, you can predict results within the limits of your objectives.
—*Air Force Manual (AFM) 35-15. Air Force Leadership, December 1948*

I had no idea what I was doing.

Standing there, in the Detachment 207 headquarters underneath the Busch Memorial Center at Saint Louis University, freshly graduated from high school. Excited to start my leadership journey, I just hoped to work hard and absorb as much as I could from those around me. I was convinced leadership success had mostly to do with pouring my heart and soul into my coursework, since that had been the measure of success in school. I didn't have a real plan for future growth. It was a major blind spot I didn't realize I had until it leapt into my consciousness right in that moment. Everyone needs a leadership development strategy, one that should start within.

Living Your Leadership[1] starts with *self-leadership* to discover, understand,

---

[1] Figure 2. * "Living your leadership" is a registered trademark of Perficitis Consulting Group, LLC.

and improve oneself. Then the focus moves to *transformational* and *servant leadership*—empathetic and follower-centric practices that complete the progression of this focused leadership strategy. Living Your Leadership enables managers to grow in their leadership practice in a deliberate and structured fashion. I will demonstrate how to develop *your* leadership style to match authentic servant leadership through individual discipline and critical reflection of character.

We strive to remain faithful to ourselves, maintain our integrity, and accept our people for who they are while recognizing both strengths and limitations. As you progress in Living Your Leadership, you will cultivate a space where every person can be genuine, feel safe, and trust one another. Living Your Leadership is something we practice not just with others but within ourselves as well.

As this book started to take shape, it became clear that it should first focus on self-knowledge as the foundation of leadership practice. Living *Your* Leadership implies a thorough understanding of self and choices that grow from that understanding. Owning your journey starts with an acknowledgment of your own characteristics and values. From self-knowledge, you can work toward an empathetic stance on leadership by shifting your focus onto others.

Dan Rockwell, one of the leadership gurus I greatly admire, said it succinctly: "The first pressing challenge of leadership is focusing on the thing that matters most. People matter most. Nurture and develop you as much as you nurture and develop others."[2] We are morally obligated to recognize that we are all humans. We wake up, work and play, and go to bed each night. Despite our economic status, title, or popularity on this earth, we are all one human family.

My leadership development started the day I arrived at orientation for Air Force Reserve Officer Training Corps (ROTC) at Saint Louis University. As I looked around at the sophomores, juniors, and seniors, I was more than intimidated; I was scared. I knew I didn't have what they had: the ability to lead, to command respect, to fill the room with their presence. As I look back on it, those whom I feared were themselves still terribly young, just beginning their journeys as well.

It was, and still is, a joyous experience to be able to learn from them. *What kind of books do they read? What meditative exercises do they practice? What are their philosophies on personal growth and team leadership?* It can be truly amazing to connect and gain insight from other leaders.

---

[2] Rockwell 2012.

Many of my leadership lessons came from my undergrad classroom professors: the Jesuits[3] who instructed me in philosophy and the arts and sciences. I learned that growth begins with an intentional focus on the self. Growing as a person, maturing in wisdom and insight, and learning about the connections between various academic fields and how theory relates to practice in so many areas was essential to my journey.

There is a wealth of readily accessible information available on self-help topics: quotes from famous people, pop psychology texts, free online courses, and more. I am more than happy to direct readers to other useful works by experts in their respective fields. Several of the topics discussed in this text are profound in their depth and impact and deserve to be explored further. As a lifelong learner, I hope that you engage with the material on a personal level.

RATHER THAN MANAGE, WE SHOULD STRIVE TO LEAD.

Transformational and servant leadership encourages leaders to inspire and cultivate their followers so they grow as people. Those followers are more likely to choose to become leaders, in turn, which inevitably benefits the entire organization. Individual leadership progress occurs when the needle moves from an internal to an external focus. Effective leadership must be built on personal integrity and character before a leader attempts to influence others.

Starting with an internal focus does not mean the leader is of any greater significance or that caring for subordinates is secondary. Rather, you have to be whole, competent, and capable of self-leadership before you engage in the awesome responsibility of leading others. Should these steps be taken out of order or performed concurrently, the result can be leadership built on a less than solid foundation. Starting the fight from a position of weakness is unwise, to paraphrase Sun Tzu[4] in his seminal work on strategy and military leadership, *The Art of War*.

Living Your Leadership emanates from a place of altruism. It stems from a clear understanding of the self, gained through critical reflection and fully manifested in servanthood.

AUTHENTICITY AND TRUST ARE THE KEYS TO ALL RELATIONSHIPS.

---

[3] Originating in sixteenth century by St. Ignatius of Loyola, a Jesuit is a member of the Society of Jesus (SJ), a Roman Catholic religious order.

[4] Tzu 1971.

Through the act of *becoming* through self-knowledge, you can consciously encourage others to be genuine, in turn. This model is not the end-all be-all; as Musashi[5] tells us, there is more than one path to the mountain's peak.[6] Unless you persevere on your journey, you will not reach that peak, regardless of the path you take.

Leadership is the bedrock of organizational effectiveness. Bryant and Kazan note that "one of the main reasons that the study of leadership development is absolutely necessary is that people with a strong sense of self lead lives that are both self-actualizing and self-transcending."[7] The journey to individual self-actualization and sincere authenticity is essential to Living Your Leadership.

The United States Air Force (USAF) and Kaiser Permanente, two distinctly different and successful organizations that depend on flexible and credible management, provided me with a unique and useful set of knowledge and experiences. As a director in the service-driven continuum of care at Kaiser Permanente,[8] a premier health care delivery system, I lead through influence, supporting hundreds of thousands of vulnerable patients and their family members. The USAF, my previous place of employment, likewise functions at the highest level of efficiency based largely upon its ever-ready middle managers.

My insights are derived and inspired from working with, as well as observing, senior executives in these operating environments. I have a great deal of experience influencing and collaboratively executing business strategies and process improvements. My passion for research has been honed by my time as a student and professor. I have been teaching in higher education for the better part of a decade, recently taking on the challenge of starting up the Masters in Human Resource Management program at Touro University Worldwide. Imbuing the pages of this text with my hard-won knowledge, I am reminded of the author of one of my favorite works of literature.

Sir Walter Scott described the perils of writing solely Scottish novels (the reading of which *is* quite perilous, as any student who has been in a literature class that featured his work can tell you) while explaining his romp into English history in his book, *Ivanhoe*:

---

[5] Miyamoto Musashi (1584–1645) was a legendary Japanese samurai and founder of the Niten-ryu sword style.

[6] Miyamoto & Harris 1974.

[7] 2013, p. 31.

[8] https://healthy.kaiserpermanente.org/.

He was not only likely to weary out the indulgence of his readers, but also greatly to limit his own power of affording them pleasure. In a highly polished country, where so much genius is monthly employed in catering for public amusement, a fresh topic, such as he had himself had the happiness to light upon, is the untasted spring of the desert: but when men and horses, cattle, camels, and dromedaries have poached the spring into mud, it becomes loathsome to those who at first drank of it with rapture; and he who had the merit of discovering it, if he would preserve his reputation with the tribe, must display his talent by a fresh discovery of untasted fountains. (Sir Walter Scott[9])

Scott's message implies that in order to keep people coming back, one must have the newest and therefore best ideas, lest the ideas become stale and as unappealing as a can of flat soda, or in Scott's case, a dried-up mud puddle from which no one wants to drink. The same can be said for the subject of leadership: people often look for the flashiest and newest idea, the idea that appeals to the latest fashion.

JUST BECAUSE SOMETHING IS SHINY AND NEW DOES NOT NECESSARILY MEAN IT IS OF VALUE.

Freshness can be said to count in things like produce, our can of soda, and the water from a natural spring. Innovation and originality are outstanding leadership traits, but leadership theories must also be steeped in knowledge of what came before. Theory should build on past practice, learned from mistakes, and grown on a foundation of success. Leadership touches all of us and can be as conceptually difficult to define as loyalty, responsibility, or honor.

While Living Your Leadership, humane treatment of others is essential. People are too often pushed to the margin and recognized solely in terms of their fiscal contributions to an organization. It is incumbent on leaders to recognize individuals are more than just cogs in the business machine. They have feelings and a sense of self-worth that is constantly at war with the persistent, negative cultural reinforcement of their identities as anonymous drones.

---

[9] Scott 1997, p. xiv–xv.

Emphasizing the intrinsic value of others and tangibly recognizing their myriad contributions renews and reinvests in your personnel. They can again see that your success, the success of your organization, and their personal success are all deeply connected. Transformational leaders know and employ methods to positively motivate and support employee morale.[10] The foundation of the practice of Living Your Leadership is to value those you lead.[11, 12]

As the legendary Jack Welch intimated in his best-selling book *Winning*,[13] the key to progressing and ultimately succeeding is understanding your particular industry from as many perspectives as possible. Understand that experience alone is not enough when it comes to leading. Experience can make a great frontline worker, but even subject matter experts need education related to their field.

LEADERSHIP IS A FIELD OF STUDY ALL ON ITS OWN.

I do not think, sir, you have any right to command me, merely
because you are older than I, or because you have seen more
of the world than I have; your claim to superiority depends
on the use you have made of your time and experience.
—Charlotte Brontë, *Jane Eyre*

A leader must be credible. They learn through multiple modalities: experience, reading, education, and socialization. As my own journey continues, I will persevere in my study of leadership. Throughout this text, you will see references to useful leadership books aligned with successful leadership theory and practice, often drawn from my Jesuit, USAF, and Kaiser experiences.

YOU SHOULD READ ABOUT LIVING YOUR LEADERSHIP.

You bought or borrowed this book, and you have read at least this far into the text. Most likely, you are a self-determining and autonomous individual. You

---

[10] Kiel and Watson 2009.
[11] Vadell and Ewing 2011.
[12] Northouse 2004.
[13] Welch and Welch 2005.

recognize the importance of leadership development and accept the idea that reading books like this one will benefit you.[14]

If you have identified the importance of study for self-improvement, perhaps you have progressed to examining yourself and have found this action to be in congruence with your values and needs. The next steps are to believe you are capable of improving, to do the hard inner work necessary to improve,[15] and to cease doubting yourself and your ability to lead.

> Our doubts are traitors,
> And make us lose the good we oft might win.
> By fearing to attempt.
> —William Shakespeare[16]

A homogeneous mixture of leadership talent or uniform knowledge is never found in any pool of employees. From an organizational standpoint, the idea behind leadership training is to increase the cumulative knowledge of a group. Training provides for a shared leadership language and improves those individual leaders who will lead the company into the future. Using a single text to align the educational efforts pushes the envelope of leadership development in a uniform direction.

In agreeing to an aligned leadership development paradigm, an organization ensures that a majority of personnel, both managers and employees, increase their knowledge level. This constitutes a virtual leadership sea change, a tidal shift that raises all ships. No one's leadership style is exactly the same as another's, but if a theoretical structure is built for anyone and everyone, it is possible to see dividends in the leadership development of an entire group.

---

[14] Ryan and Deci 2000.
[15] George 2015.
[16] *Measure for Measure*, act 1, scene 4.

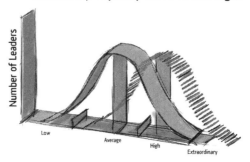

**Leadership Development Shifts the
Leadership Capacity Curve to the Right**

Number of Leaders

Low

Average

High

Extraordinary

Leadership Capacity

Figure 1. Improving organizational leadership competency

The notion of 'leadership capacity' is extremely important. It is not simply a function of the number or quality of individuals in formal leadership roles, rather, it implies a system of leadership, if you will, that can ignite leadership wisdom, insight, and behaviors from many more individuals. Thus it fuels the continuing search for different kinds of leadership approaches, both individual and joint, at all levels of the organization. In fact, many downsizing, restructuring, and reengineering efforts are actually reducing the number of leadership and management positions in the formal structure. The objective function of all this is to expand the capacity for leadership and independent initiative without having to increase the number of individuals in formal leadership roles. (Jon R. Katzenbach[17])

THE MODEL: LIVING YOUR LEADERSHIP

There are as many leadership models as there are recipes for chili in Texas. Living Your Leadership combines carefully curated exigent theories; it is an

---

[17] Katzenbach 1997, p. 84.

organic and grounded model that relies on theory but is meant to be put into daily practice.

Figure 2. The Living Your Leadership theoretical framework

Leadership development should include a theoretical framework. A theoretical framework is something leaders use to define their personal leadership styles and inform their leadership interactions. In most cases, the theoretical framework, even those advertised as solve-all models, are not flexible enough and do not take into account the emotional and organically evolving realities of the real world.

Living Your Leadership employs a unique, holistic approach that encourages authentically aligned behaviors informed by the theories outlined in this text. The Living Your Leadership paradigm incorporates primarily the tenets of self-leadership, transformational leadership, and servant leadership. This paradigm offers a highly *individualized* path to developing leaders.

The uniqueness of the model is predicated on the development of a leader's personal traits and characteristics during the mastery of self-leadership. It also provides a sounding board for accomplished leaders with the tacit understanding anyone *can*[18] lead but not just anyone *should*. It recognizes that as people mature, their motivations move from a carrot-and-stick, external motivational context to an intrinsic orientation.[19]

Decision-making processes grow more self-directing over time in

---

[18] Sinek 2011.
[19] Chandler and Connell 1987.

accordance with a natural need to be autonomous.[20] This process of internalization yields adaptive[21] social advantages and enhanced well-being.[22] Living Your Leadership infuses traditional leadership philosophies with the most current research in leadership to help individuals mature.

---

[20] Ryan 1995.
[21] Ryan, Kuhl, and Deci 1997.
[22] Ryan and Deci 2000.

Conquer yourself and the world is at your feet.
—Saint Augustine

LEADING YOURSELF

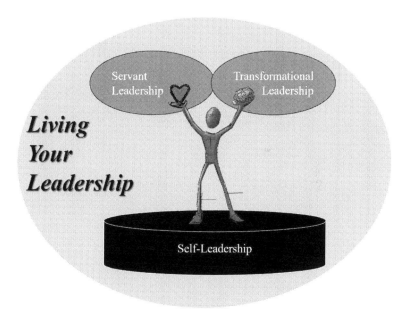

GROW INTENTIONALLY

Most of the significant things done in the world were done by
persons who were either too busy or too sick! There are few
ideal and leisurely settings for the disciplines of growth.
– Robert Thornton Henderson [23]

My active duty time in the USAF launched in the nuclear missile field.
Smartphones weren't a thing yet, and you weren't allowed to bring devices
that could store or transmit information onto the missile site. To keep track
of what happened on our shifts, missileers kept an unclassified journal called
an alert log. Our shifts ranged from twenty-four to seventy-two hours on site,
and we called theses shifts "alerts." A two- or three-person team manned the
launch control site from which intercontinental nuclear missiles were targeted
and could be launched at the direction of the president.

Captain Jimmy Winters took me on my first alert. The drive to any alert
facility from the military base was a minimum of forty-five minutes one way
with nothing to see but snowy plains in the winter and well-tilled fields in the
summer. After a few trips across the Northern Tier plains, the novelty started
to wane. The long trips with little else to occupy the time meant the two crew
members always had a great deal of time to talk. Capt. Winters was a solid
mentor who believed in training his deputy crew commanders by first getting
to know them. He used these long drives as a time to do just that.

---

[23] American author, pastor, and Presbyterian denominational leader.

My first trip out to the site was an overwhelming experience. I was nervous about memorizing the security phrases we needed to transmit over the radio before being allowed to drive through the gate onto the complex. Capt. Winters rehearsed the verbiage with me over and over before I had to make our radio call. My voice quavered a bit, but we got onto the site successfully. We checked in with the machine gun-toting security controller and rode down the industrial elevator to the capsule for the first time. The solemn weight of isolation seemed to increase as it creakily descended the fifty feet into the junction between the launch control center (LCC) and the launch control equipment building. For the uninitiated, it was like entering a buried, prehistoric starship. The sights and faintly chemical smells, the oppressive darkness broken by intermittent incandescent bulbs. It was eerie.

The crew worked out of the launch control center[24] and were responsible for carefully checking and maintaining the attached structure holding the equipment that sustained basic functions of air, power, and water for the underground capsule. There were two eight-ton blast doors formed of solid steel and concrete. One door led from the elevator into the junction between the launch control center and the equipment building, and the other led directly into the LCC where the off-going crew was waiting to be relieved.

The sequential blast doors served a dual purpose: they protected the crew and equipment from blast overpressure and provided security against hostile intrusion. The first door was hand operated by a spinning a manual crank and then using a latch. I nervously worked the hand crank on the blast door, and it silently and grudgingly swung open, expelling a gust of stale air.

After we conducted a thorough crew changeover, when the off-going crew and the oncoming crew verified classified material disposition and signed over control of the facility and its associated nuclear warheads, I was officially on my first alert.

Capt. Winters and I went over various checklists and procedures for several hours and then settled in to watch some B movies before he took his turn in the bed-mod: the coffin-sized, curtained enclosure where one of the two ICBM[25] crew members was allowed a modest amount of privacy and sleep during predetermined rest periods.

I vividly remember being scared to death that I would mess up a seemingly insignificant detail and ruin my career before it even started. Thankfully that

---

[24] For a more detailed description of the facilities: http://npshistory.com/publications/mimi/srs/sites.htm.

[25] Intercontinental ballistic missile.

didn't happen. In my time at Minot AFB, I pulled over three hundred of these alerts during a three-year period.

When I reached out to Jimmy on social media and asked what he remembered about our time together in the missile field, he replied, "The thing I remember most about you was your drive. You were different than most. You had a clear vision of the path you wanted to take and where you wanted to end up. I remember talking to you in the office about your goals and what you wanted to accomplish."

He went on to say it is a leader's responsibility to accept the personal ambitions of followers, that the leader must encourage followers in their development. He believed in never cutting corners on the path to self-development. He taught me then the importance of giving my best, never losing focus on my goals, which allowed me to establish perspective. Jimmy encouraged me then that wherever I saw chances to learn and grow, even if others only saw them as distractions, I should avidly pursue them.

> Change is inevitable. Growth is optional.
> —John Maxwell

In the course of my professional and personal life, I have experienced very little free time to sit back and reflect, to take the time to read professional literature and apply those principles in a low-stress environment. There hasn't been a time in my adult life I haven't worked at least two jobs and had a family to care for. The man I chose to be my dissertation mentor decided to accept the position as chair of my dissertation committee because he remembered I had taken his class during my combat deployment to Mosul, Iraq. I suppose he figured if I could pass social psychology under those conditions, researching and writing a dissertation would be a piece of cake.

Despite how difficult it has been to carve out time for critical reflection, I recognized the value of choosing to make the time. Fitting reflection into my daily schedule gave me the chance to think about the choices I'd made that day, to consider their outcomes and antecedents, and to incorporate contemplative understanding into my mindfulness practice.

Reflection is crucial to the practice of mindfulness. One of the major benefits of a mindfulness practice is being present in the moment, to accept circumstances as they are and to recognize the opportunities for growth and joy in our lives. Our minds tend to wander many of our waking hours, but the practice of mindfulness allows our minds to slow down. Constant demands on our attention, from smart devices to emails to meetings and appointments, clutter our consciousness. Mindfulness encourages focus, improving our decision-making capability and easing our stress. I've learned that leaders should always take advantage of the present moment. That they should learn and grow intentionally. It is through intentional striving that leaders thrive in all environments, from nuclear launch facilities to deployments in Iraq.

CONSCIOUSLY COMMIT TO YOUR PERSONAL GROWTH.

Learning is not attained by chance,
it must be sought for with ardor and attended to with diligence.

—Abigail Adams

For leaders, time for relevant reflection must be built into the day, at the beginning or the end. Reflection allows the leader time to organize short-term priorities, to prioritize daily actions, and to validate the coherence between inner desires and outward decisions. Demands on our time are ever present, especially in our data-driven, technologically advanced workplaces. Managers today are required to know more, to have access to more information, and to interact faster and yet meaningfully with employees. You *have* time to develop your leadership, though you will most likely have to *make* the time.

Time is an equal opportunity employer.
Each human being has exactly the same number
of hours and minutes every day.
Rich people can't buy more hours.
Scientists can't invent new minutes.
And you can't save time to spend it on another day.
Even so, time is amazingly fair and forgiving.
No matter how much time you've wasted in the past,
you still have an entire tomorrow.
—Denis Waitley[26]

Remember that diamonds are nothing more than lumps of coal that persevered through the heat and pressure:

---

[26] International best-selling author, consultant, and motivational speaker.

Just as the diamond requires properties for its formation—carbon, heat, and pressure—successful leaders require the interaction of three properties—character, knowledge, and application. Like carbon to a diamond, character is the basic quality of a leader ... But as carbon alone does not create a diamond; neither can character alone create a leader. The diamond needs heat. Man needs knowledge, study, and preparation ... The third property, pressure,—acting in conjunction with carbon and heat—forms the diamond. Similarly, one's character attended by knowledge, blooms through application to produce a leader. (General Edward C. Meyer[27])

The law of intentionality describes growth as an active process. It is not something that *just happens*; rather, it is something that is *intentionally* pursued. John Maxwell's[28] *15 Invaluable Laws of Growth*[29] outlines the law of intentionality as having several traps. He describes these traps as gaps in our perception that stop us from becoming our best selves or from making crucial decisions.

For example, the assumption gap is the idea you will grow without any real effort. However, critical reflection and discernment are necessary for growth. The knowledge gap says you don't necessarily know *how* to grow; you go about your day-to-day life without having to worry about the question "How do I improve myself?" or "What are the steps required to become a better person and a better leader?" The knowledge gap can easily be addressed by reading some of the excellent books out there. Finally, the timing gap: the idea there is an easier time to grow than right now. We all face these gaps, knowingly or unknowingly.

The practice of Living Your Leadership addresses these gaps head-on, allowing the leader to grow with intentionality and direction.

There are no office hours for leaders.
—Cardinal J. Gibbons[30]

---

[27] US Army chief of staff, 1979–1983.
[28] John C. Maxwell is a *NYT* best-selling author and leadership guru. He has sold more than twenty-six million books in fifty languages and has trained more than six million leaders.
[29] Maxwell 2014.
[30] Archbishop of Baltimore (1834–1921).

A lack of intentionality and personal accountability are two reasons many people who lead busy and happy lives do not stretch themselves and develop their potential fully. They tell themselves tomorrow will be easier and the next day they will have X, Y, or Z done. Or they say they are far too busy just now to worry about this (seemingly) immense challenge in their lives. Perhaps they believe that success will just happen, refusing to acknowledge their personal agency in their lives. Adopting a defeatist attitude, a person may consider the steps to success so large as to make the climb impossible. My hope is, as you read this book, you will realize the only possible kind of steps are small but not insignificant steps.

A paradigm shift is not achieved instantaneously upon the acquisition of new information. Becoming the leader you hope to be is a revelatory and often difficult journey. This challenge will not come to a resolution in a day or a month or even a year. It is a gradual process through which we develop as authentic and active leaders. Even aha moments do not typically occur without self-reflection and prior knowledge playing a large role.

> There is a simple realization from which all personal improvement and growth emerges. This is the realization that we, individually, are responsible for everything in our lives, no matter the external circumstances. We don't always control what happens to us. But we always control how we interpret what happens to us, as well as how we respond. Whether we consciously recognize it or not, we are always responsible for our experiences. It's impossible not to be. Choosing to not consciously interpret events in our lives is still an interpretation of the events of our lives. (Mark Manson[31])

Take time to read leadership books and blogs, to listen to podcasts, attend seminars, lectures, and conferences,[32] and to connect with other managers. Spend that extra few minutes a day encouraging your employees, using the techniques you learn. All of these practices are essential. Leadership growth activities are more valuable pursuits when considered together than they seem to be individually. Improving yourself and improving your work environment pays dividends significantly greater than the effort it takes. Use your infrequent

---

[31] 2016, p. 94.
[32] Pfeffer and Sutton 2000.

free moments. Build small islands of deliberation. Meditate on your actions and your plans. Engage with your followers on a more profound level. These small steps lead to self-development, collaboration, and solidarity.

> Personal development is a belief that you are worth the
> effort, time, and energy to develop yourself.
> —Denis Waitley

Leadership development should not start right from the *leading others* aspect of leadership. It is a grave error to skip over what is a truly rich and underappreciated foundational issue: development of self. Leadership training that does not emphasize critical reflection is shallow. Without critical reflection, disciplined thought, and understanding of yourself, it is not possible to change your own core attributes and ensure authentic interactions with others.

The conscious act of *being authentic* can preclude attaining authenticity.[33] In the attempt to *seem* authentic, a leader puts on a persona that they hope will mimic their perception of their ideal leader. These leaders have not taken the time to critically reflect. They refuse to do the hard, small steps, the necessary work of developing authenticity from the inside out. Rather than trying to *seem* authentic, you should *be* authentic. Authentic action is grounded in your individuality, it is animated by your character, and informed by your lived experience.

> Those who try to make life better for everyone without having learned to
> control their own lives first usually end up making things worse all around.
> —Mihaly Csikszentmihalyi[34]

The glaringly obvious issue, in this particular progression, are those leadership courses that do not begin with an understanding of the individual, of the self. Positive self-efficacy beliefs start with an evaluation of yourself and acknowledgment of your self-worth; self-esteem[35] and building that self-esteem serves as the foundation of self-leadership.[36] Psychological and psychosocial issues are often amplified in leadership positions based on the fact that leaders are visible to their subordinates in all of their actions.

---

[33] Caza and Jackson 2011.
[34] 1990, p. 191. Dr. Csikszentmihalyi is a distinguished professor of psychology and management founder, codirector, Quality of Life Research Center (QLRC).
[35] Rosenberg 1979.
[36] Bryant and Kazan 2013, p. 32.

7

If a leader is a narcissist, their narcissism is on display if they are the leader of a group. Conversely, a leader possessed of a humble, compassionate nature will be recognized as well. "Self-leaders, therefore, live by a mantra—'there is no failure, only feedback for improvement'—because they have the confidence that they learn from mistakes and move forward."[37] This mantra should extend throughout one's organization. All levels of personnel should have access to clear and concise feedback and be treated fairly in the context of *learning from mistakes and moving forward*.

As you continue your self-improvement journey, keep in mind that resiliency is a key trait in self-improvement. There are always solutions to problems, though they may not immediately present themselves or have a totally satisfactory resolution. Additionally, problems sometimes linger. Issues you are working on may not be resolved in a time frame anyone thinks is reasonable.

> Do not try to excuse your faults, try to correct them.
>
> —Saint Giovanni "Don" Bosco

Your improvement journey may take a number of years; some say the self-improvement journey never ends. With specific milestones in mind, it will be easier to judge your progress along the way. When the going gets tough, the resilience you have developed will allow you to face difficulties. You will learn to thrive under internal and external pressure, making mistakes and celebrating successes. Part of growing in resilience is being able to learn from your failures.

> A human being is not one thing among others; things determine each other, but man is ultimately self-determining. What he becomes—within the limits of endowment and environment—he has made out of himself. In the concentration camps, for example, in this living laboratory and on this testing ground, we watched and witnessed some of our comrades behave like swine while others behaved like saints. Man has both potentialities within himself; which one is actualized depends on decisions but not on conditions. (Viktor E. Frankl[38])

---

[37] Bryant and Kazan 2013, p. 69.
[38] 1963, p. 157.

CHAPTER RECAP

Consciously commit to personal growth. It is an active and intentional process.

- Make the time to reflect, especially when it is difficult.
- Ingest material that will aid your personal growth journey by reading leadership books and blogs, listening to podcasts, and attending seminars, lectures, and conferences.
- Connect with other managers and respected leaders. Ask probing questions and notice the areas where you differ from them in practice and in character.
- Encourage your employees using the techniques you learn. Practical application is key.
- Do not expect immediate results. Personal change takes time and effort.

TEMET NOSCE

The key to becoming an effective leader is not to focus on making other people follow, but on making yourself the kind of person they want to follow.
—John C. Maxwell

I was bereft.

The airplane trip to St. Louis from Sacramento on TWA seemed like I had been shoved through a portal onto a different planet. I had no friends. I was one of only a handful of students from the West Coast who had been admitted to Saint Louis University. ROTC was only one day per week, but even that marginally social activity seemed intimidating to a newly displaced introvert.

Naturally, I clung to what I knew; I clung to what I had previous mastery experiences in that had informed my self-concept. I excelled in my studies. Upon entering my philosophy classroom on the first day of school, I found it was a traditional lecture hall setup, just like I had seen in the movies! Our professor, a seemingly ancient Jesuit priest, greeted us warmly as we entered. He started our first lecture of the semester with the story of the oracle at Delphi and the principle of *temet nosce*.[39]

We spent the next several weeks deconstructing our conscious and unconscious cultural biases. We learned to question all of our previously lived

---

[39] *Temet nosce* or "know thyself" is a Latin translation of a popular ancient maxim traced back to ancient Egypt and chiseled in stone on the Temple of Apollo at Delphi in Greece.

experiences. We were taught to critically examine those experiences and our previously held beliefs. We learned to see our lives and our beliefs anew, as through a lens of critical self-reflection. We worked to evaluate and incorporate them into our newly emerging understanding of self. The geographically enforced isolation, coupled with the Jesuit philosophical training, kick-started my process of self-understanding.

Self-leadership is the theory underpinning Living Your Leadership. It requires "having a developed sense of who you are, what you can do, and where you are going coupled with the ability to influence your communication, emotions, and behavior on the way to getting there."[40] A foundational understanding in self-leadership practice is that leaders can be grown and nurtured.[41] Though certain desirable leadership traits might naturally occur in certain people, the lack of an inborn propensity toward leadership is not a barrier to the rest of us developing and enhancing our own leadership characteristics through study and practice.

A leader who truly values people makes a deliberate choice to behave as a servant. The choice to serve is grounded in "an accurate understanding of his or her self-image, moral conviction and emotional stability."[42] His Holiness the Dalai Lama recognized there has been a lack of inner development in the last fifty years. People rarely consider compassion, spirituality, and humanity's inner life, preferring instead to focus on the external signs and symbols of success.[43]

> Lack of self-knowledge and failure to appreciate one's own worth make for faulty judgement in all other matters; If you are not able to understand (and accept) your own self, you will not be able to understand (or accept) what is beyond you.
> —Saint Bonaventure [44]

Understanding your own strengths, weaknesses, belief system, and motivations is the only way to master self-leadership. You have to know yourself before you can lead yourself. You have to be able to lead yourself before you

---

[40] Bryant and Kazan 2013, p. 85.
[41] Thompson 1995.
[42] Sendjaya and Sarros 2002.
[43] Bstan-'dzin-rgya-mtsho 2011.
[44] A Franciscan in medieval Italy, Giovanni di Fidanza was a scholastic theologian and philosopher.

can be expected to lead others. Developing a thorough understanding of the emotional self is a purposeful and deliberate process.

The path to understanding takes stamina and determination since it involves an evolutionary change. Each piece of understanding builds upon the last. Self-knowledge is one of the most important tangible assets of a leader.[45] The concept of self-leadership purposefully mirrors what it takes to effectively lead others: understanding, effort, and focus. Living Your Leadership requires a compassionate and empathetic connection with your followers. It stands to reason you would need a compassionate and empathetic connection with yourself before you are prepared to offer that part of yourself to others.

The idea of being compassionate with yourself may sound silly initially. Compassion flows from one person to another, doesn't it? As an exercise to demonstrate how someone can be compassionate to oneself, take a moment and try to think of times when you have not been especially kind to yourself. Were you angry or sad about something, an event or a situation, but you did not know exactly why? Have you ever used negative self-talk when you feel like you failed at something? Positive self-talk is an important skill to develop.[46] Nailing an employee to the wall for a mistake is not an effective motivational technique, and it does not do much for you either. Be willing to forgive your own mistakes.

> The greatest of faults, I should say, is to be conscious of none.
> —Thomas Carlyle [47]

Identify your personal faults, be willing to do the hard work to mitigate them, and be constantly and consistently willing to forgive yourself for not fulfilling your own mental model of the perfect leader. As a technique to prevent mistakes in future judgment, condemnation does not encourage followership, other than perhaps out of fear.

---

[45] Montgomery III 2007.
[46] Figure 3.
[47] Scottish philosopher, satirist, historian, and teacher (1795–1881).

Figure 3. Self-talk loop

Fear is a poor motivational tactic.[48] It employs psychological bullying and often results in decreased motivation and loyalty after its initial effects wear off. This fact is true when it comes to the self as well. You will not encourage yourself to examine issues causing mistakes through self-degradation. Negative self-talk will not change your habitual thinking; it will only make you feel bad and start to solidify a lack of self-esteem, which will invariably crush developing leadership attributes.

FEW THINGS ARE MORE HARMFUL THAN NEGATIVE SELF-TALK.

Behavior flows from our thoughts. Self-recriminatory thoughts produce hesitant behavior. Hesitant behavior then causes the mind to anticipate failure. Anticipating failure makes it more likely that you will fail, since behavior flows from thoughts. It is a destructive cycle.

Forgive your mistakes rather than using negative self-talk. Resolve to correct behavior that failed to meet expectations and move on. Practice compassion with yourself by generously forgiving your own mistakes. Forgiveness creates a safe mental space to learn from those mistakes. Without a safe mental environment, it is easy to devolve into the cycle of self-recrimination.

---

[48] Treasurer 2014.

Man is now not only a social being;
his social nature transcends national and regional limits,
and whether we like it or not,
we must think in terms of one human family,
one world.

—Thomas Merton [49]

The lenses with which we view ourselves and the world around us are often shaped by our differences rather than by what makes us similar. The Dalai Lama notes there are many aspects to focus on when we view others. There are so many things that make people different: race, gender, religion, national origin, occupation, and level of education. These tangible characteristics moderate the way we interact with our social environment. Focusing on visible differences to the exclusion of that which brings us together negatively influences behavior toward *the other*.[50]

Rather than focusing on all of the things that make people different, turn your lens on our common humanity. People too often see external characteristics and stop thinking. This lazy thinking places the cognitive emphasis on ourselves. We attend to that which makes us different, rather than what we have in common—our ability to love and our desire to forgive, to love, and be loved.

There is nothing wrong with recognizing the differences between people, just as there is nothing wrong with identifying and internalizing those immutable characteristics that influence our self-concept. Failing to recognize the individual makeup of others shows a lack of empathy. It is through recognizing and respecting[51] the inherent dignity of others that we are united. We share our human dignity, regardless of our physical characteristics.

RESPECTING OUR SHARED HUMAN DIGNITY RAISES A LEADER ABOVE COMMON PETTINESS.

Respecting others is a crucial aspect of leadership development.[52] Considering others and our interconnectedness inexorably shifts the focus from our own

---

[49] A Trappist monk, poet, and social activist (1915–1968).
[50] Bstan-'dzin-rgya-mtsho 2011.
[51] De Pree 1989.
[52] Firth-Cozens and Mowbray 2001.

interests to compassion for all people. We acknowledge that for one of us to succeed, we all must succeed. This frame of thought encourages empathy and increases our ability to self-lead with compassion.

> The most important single ingredient in the formula of
> success is knowing how to get along with people.
> —Theodore Roosevelt

Good leaders tend to be highly emotionally intelligent. According to Daniel Goleman,[53] emotional intelligence (EQ) is both established at birth and can be learned. His research strongly suggests there is a genetic component to emotional intelligence. Psychological research in the field of human developmental indicates nurturing plays a role in growing empathy and other-centeredness, which are hallmarks of EQ.

Emotional intelligence increases with study and with life experience. Developing EQ causes us to grow as people, to accept ourselves, and to more fully align our inner beliefs with our outer behavior.

> What we achieve inwardly will change outer reality.
> —Plutarch

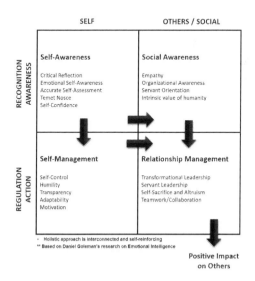

Figure 4. Emotional intelligence

---

[53] 2004.

The Dalai Lama identifies compassion as a foundational human emotion. He insists that compassion can be learned through experience[54] and that, through compassion, ethical behavior can be informed and practiced. By engaging in literature, reflection, meditation, and connecting with others, empathy is increased. Extensive social contact with people who are different from us facilitates an understanding of the diversity of emotions and experiences others experience. Compassion is developed through shared understanding and social experience.

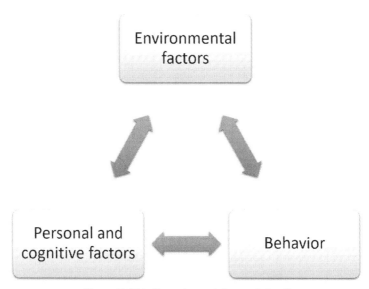

Figure 5. Triadic reciprocal determinism[55]

Albert Bandura's theory of social cognition[56] was a groundbreaking way to understand the cause of behaviors in the context of a reciprocal model. Human behavior had before been explained as resulting from a single causal factor, either environment or internal dispositions.[57] In triadic[58] reciprocal determinism, behavior is influenced by cognitive and environmental factors. The interaction between a person and their environment determines behavior, as does the influence of a person's internal characteristics. Behavior shaped

---

[54] Bstan-'dzin-rgya-mtsho 2011.
[55] Bandura 1978.
[56] Bandura 1986.
[57] Bandura 1989.
[58] Three closely interrelated factors.

by this reciprocal determinism informs the beliefs that a person develops. Therefore, beliefs are inextricably linked to the social environment.

Table 1. Positive leadership attributes

Self-Awareness	Understanding one's emotions, strengths, weaknesses,[1] and driving forces; they are neither overly critical nor unrealistically hopeful; they are honest to self and others; they are self-regulating; they have an inner conversation with the self, helping to keep emotions and feelings under control or in check.
Motivation	Driven to achieve beyond expectations of themselves and others; they are full of passion for what they do, achieve, or learn.
Social Skills	They have the ability to communicate and to authentically interact with others; they find common ground with almost everyone.
Empathy	The ability to understand the emotional makeup of others; they are thoughtful and understanding of others' feelings.[2]

There is a distinct lack of studies quantifying the detriment or benefit of emotional intelligence to an organization; such studies are often focused on too many variables to return unmixed findings. Some highly emotionally intelligent leaders may be manipulative and use their abilities for personal achievement or organizational gain with little attention to social responsibility.[59] The relationship between EQ, moral reasoning, and ethical behavior is a question for potentially fruitful research.

It seems apparent that how EQ is used by leadership within an organization is dependent on the individual. The leader's moral worldview and organizational cultural beliefs should be in close alignment to forgo the possibility of ethically questionable leadership behavior. Morals are often culturally defined and black and white.[60] Ethics involves the reasoned approach to moral conundrums. There are several artifices and formulas[61] for

---

[59] Sivanathan and Fekken 2002.
[60] Morals are axiomatic to the individual. That is, they are self-evident. This is why morals tend to vary depending on social norms.
[61] Examples include Aristotelian, Kantian, utilitarian, Nichomachean, and virtue ethics.

determining the ethical disposition of a situation or a decision. This is why ethics can be examined and debated, but axiomatic truths tend to be regarded as sacrosanct depending on cultural context.

Here again we see the connection between leadership and an individual's values. One must understand one's own belief system before attempting to lead others.

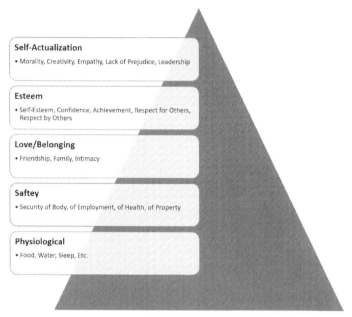

Figure 6. Modified Maslow's hierarchy of needs[62]

You cannot reach a level of self-actualization, whatever your interpretation of the hierarchy of needs, by relying on others to get you there. As children, we are provided with the first few levels by our caregivers. It is up to us to develop ourselves and seek the good of others to continue the climb. Self-actualization is a level of the hierarchy that must be developed internally through success, mastery experiences, and by learning from failures over time. Being aided in the journey toward self-actualization by effective mentorship allows leaders to ascend the hierarchy more efficiently.[63]

Ideally, individuals move through their lives with a consistent approach

---

[62] The hierarchy of needs is a popular theory in psychology that was originally proposed by Abraham Maslow in 1943.

[63] Burns 1978.

to self-actualization.[64] Chemers, Watson, and May claim "high levels of dispositional confidence and optimism, [are] gained through graduated success experiences that help to build such self-perceptions."[65] In many cases, we take steps away from self-actualization with negative self-talk and failing to learn the right lessons from setbacks; traumatic experiences can also be detrimental to self-actualization if they are not dealt with in a healthy and therapeutic manner. Convincing yourself not to lie to yourself is difficult, and you can fall back into it easily. Additionally, asking for help from a mental health or mentoring professional, or for support from one's network, is never a bad thing.

Arrogance has often been described in a negative light, but it is, in many cases, nothing more or less than self-confidence fearlessly presenting itself via outward expression. Socially acceptable pride is a rare thing; it can be inspiring and enervating. When a person has self-confidence, when they have high self-esteem, they are more likely to be high achievers. A healthy dose of self-confidence is necessary in good leaders.

Living Your Leadership requires self-confidence and self-respect. Self-respect is a prerequisite for earning the respect of others. How can you respect and desire to follow an individual who does not have confidence in themselves? Confidence is achieved through the recognition and celebration of your personal strengths and positive attributes but only after deeply questioning yourself to understand your faults. In the continual search for humble, approachable, credible leaders,[66] we may discredit authoritative, confident individuals. The prideful approach to leadership is never to be desired; rather, a leader should recognize and respect the innate value of all people, being willing to humbly serve. That is the line between confidence and arrogance. An arrogant leader believes in themselves to a fault. The opinions of others are not valued by the arrogant leader. A confident leader, on the other hand, seeks meaningful feedback. They feel deeply that they are meant to serve, rather than be served.

Leadership is not a state of being but actions taken by individual people. You are only as leaderly as the last action you took. Even if your last action was a mistake, owning that mistake is a leaderly decision. Leaders are built, not born. They are formed from the constant pressure and refinement consisting of the actions they have taken and the lessons they have learned from those actions.

Whether leadership is good or bad often depends on the receptiveness of

---

[64] Maslow 1943.
[65] Chemers, Watson, and May 2000, p. 274.
[66] Motto of the USAF Weapons School at Nellis AFB, NV.

a person to learning new approaches, engaging in and integrating feedback and their level of authenticity.[67] Self-awareness is the precursor and the foundation of authenticity. It is impossible to be your authentic self if you do not possess self-knowledge.

---

[67] http://brenebrown.com/videos/.

CHAPTER RECAP

Knowing yourself is necessary in order to lead yourself. Leading yourself is a prerequisite to leading others.

- Understand your own strengths, weaknesses, belief system, and motivations.
- Give yourself time and compassion. Develop positive self-talk to build upon self-image and result in complementary actions.
- Work to understand and grow your emotional intelligence. Starting with self-awareness and regulation, EQ encourages positive social interactions and is a key enabler for effective and compassionate leadership practices.
- Recognize that beliefs and actions are informed by your environment.
- Healthy pride should not be confused with egotism or arrogance. An appreciation of self applies to the esteem category of Maslow's hierarchy.

INTEGRITY AND MENTORSHIP

> Show me a successful individual and I'll show you someone
> who had real positive influences in his or her life. I don't care
> what you do for a living—if you do it well I'm sure there was
> someone cheering you on or showing the way. A mentor.
> —Denzel Washington

My wife was bone weary and scared that night, as she had been almost every single day for months. Our infant son was sick. We had been told by a specialist that he needed to be seen out of state. The base's lead pediatrician, acting as the base hospital commander, refused to send him. During the prayer meeting, the kind wife of a high-ranking officer recommended that we speak to my commander to see what could be done.

The emotional toll of my son's illness on our family was indescribable. We were helpless to get him the treatment he needed. My commander was a man of great integrity. You could always go to Lieutenant Colonel Jed Davis with anything, and he would really listen. I met with Lt. Col. Davis the next day. He immediately went into action on our behalf. He recognized that we had tried to solve the problem ourselves and that we'd reached the limit of what we were able to do on our own. Although we never heard the full details, after a meeting between the hospital commander and Lt. Col. Davis, she immediately signed the paperwork to get our son the treatment he needed. In the space of a week we went from being completely helpless to having special medical orders to a specialty hospital across the country. Lt. Col. Davis acted with integrity and grit, saving my son's life.

None of the principles outlined in these pages exist in a vacuum. A precursor to servanthood is humility. A prerequisite to productive critical reflection is being a person of integrity, and integrity is more than just rule-following. A person of integrity acts in a predictable manner that is dictated by the alignment of their values and actions.

> Leadership is a potent combination of strategy and character.
> But if you must be without one, be without the strategy.
> —Norman Schwarzkopf

Take a minute and try something in your workplace. Ask your peers to define *integrity*. You will learn there are many different ways to define this simple word. Many leaders believe others should know what this word means, but there always seems to be significant variation. Why is this?

The United States military is an outstanding organization that places incredible value on leadership. The United States Air Force lists integrity as its primary core value. Unfortunately, the definition of this desirable trait is subject to dispute. One of the more common, sarcastic comments one often hears about *integrity first* in the air force is that *integrity* is a force that holds objects together.[68] Though this notion is tongue-in-cheek, it actually draws attention to an important point: trait words are not as specifically defined as they should be.

> If a good reputation is like gold,
> then having integrity is like owning the mine.
> —John C. Maxwell

General Lorenz described integrity in terms of the strength of a building. He noted that the USAF as an institution is built on the collective strength of its members' integrity. He wrote those words during a difficult political climate in the USAF. Despite difficult times, some leaders rise to the occasion and embody, rather than simply exhibit, transparent and just leadership behaviors.

---

[68] Like electromagnetic structural integrity or tissue integrity; integrity as a physical descriptor, rather than a moral characteristic.

Having served under Colonel Davis, I know that he shares General Lorenz's perspective that transparency is foundational to integrity.[69]

> Excellent leaders stand for absolute
> integrity, absolute honesty. They
> preach the concept of honesty in the
> organization. Excellent leaders practice
> integrity in thought, word, and
> deed. And they insist upon integrity
> and honesty on the part of their subordinates.
> —General W. L. Creech [70]

Acting with integrity is often described as doing the right thing when no one is looking and not doing the wrong thing when no one is looking. But what is the right thing? How do we define the right thing? The right thing, it can be argued, is culturally or situationally dependent. No book of rules or flowchart can adequately capture the entire realm of leadership experience that would dictate what the *right thing* would be in any given circumstance. Millennia of ethics scholars have tried, and we still do not have consensus. At least in the case of the air force, the right thing can often be recognized through the lens of regulations and technical orders, the organizational mission, and the rules of engagement. In a nonmilitary setting, things can get even more convoluted with regard to *what is right*.

Acting with integrity informs a culture of transparency in an organization. When a leader is predictably ethical, when they act in accordance with obvious principles, they are likely to be perceived as just. It is uncomfortable being scrutinized, but being open to criticism and having your methods and character on display allow for more authentic interactions. A transparent leader is a humble leader.

> My advice to new leaders is this:
> if you want to be a good leader, start by being a good person.
> Leadership is an inside job.
> Before you can lead people outwardly, you have to lead yourself inwardly.
> Leadership starts with internal goodness, in other words, integrity.
> —Bill Treasurer [71]

---

[69] Lorenz 2012.

[70] General Wilbur Lyman Creech commanded the USAF Tactical Air Command, 1978–1984.

[71] International best-selling author and chief encouragement officer at Giant Leap Consulting.

Fairness reflects on the leader but also means that the direction the organization is taking is transparent. Secrets are not guarded, their use in political power plays are curtailed, and cooperation is increased when the leader is able to articulate their philosophy through consistent, ethical action. "Public opinion is a weak tyrant compared with our own private opinion. What a man thinks of himself, that it is which determines, or rather indicates, his fate."[72] Integrity is a very personal matter. A leader acting with integrity acts in accordance with their internal, predefined set of morals and values.[73]

> The supreme quality for leadership is unquestionably integrity.
> Without it, no real success is possible, no matter whether it is on
> a section gang, a football field, in an army, or in an office.
> —Dwight D. Eisenhower

A seasoned leader has lived experiences and knowledge, which have provided opportunities for growth and insight. Crucibles are described as a place, time, or situation characterized by the confluence of powerful intellectual, social, economic, or political forces;[74] a crucible is a severe test of patience, belief, or both.[75] The term crucible refers to intense and meaningful experiences that leaders continually draw from to gain insight.[76] There are four types of crucibles: (1) mentoring relationships, (2) enforced reflection, (3) insertion into foreign territory, and (4) disruption or loss. The leader does not look at a crucible as a tragic event but as a learning experience, an opportunity. True leaders see what they can learn from crucibles, not how to use them as a reeking pond of self-pity in which to wallow.

Leaders with integrity need four character strengths: consistency, honesty, morality, and trustworthiness. Leaders with integrity show how consistent they are in their actions and words and always show who they are and what they stand for when faced with difficult trials.

> The immediate influence of behavior is always
> more effective than that of words.
> —Viktor Frankl [77]

---

[72] Thoreau and Levin, p. 10–11.
[73] George 2015.
[74] De Pree 1989.
[75] Bennis and Thomas 2002a.
[76] Bennis and Thomas 2002a.
[77] 1963, p. 101.

Leaders at the top of the organization are figureheads who should be role models demonstrating organizational values. Leaders with integrity also demonstrate the following: bravery, having the strength to speak up even when opposition exists;[78] perspective, understanding the strengths and weaknesses of their competitors; and social intelligence, sensing what makes themselves and others tick.[79] Many leaders will show bravery and stay true to their values, which makes them stronger than most; they must also have courage to stand alone when it is necessary.[80]

It can be difficult to maintain your principles in the face of pressures from your superiors or your subordinates. Bill George[81] warns leaders not to be swayed by expediency in the face of that external pressure. Taking a traditional view, Bill advises that a leader should ignore the prevailing wisdom, not following the crowd. That a leader should take care to adjust their methods slowly over time to best suit their own *true north*.[82]

Regard your soldiers as your children,
and they will follow you into the deepest valleys;
look on them as your own beloved sons,
and they will stand by you even unto death.
—Sun Tzu

Team members are not Amazon.com packages. Followers do not come with gift receipts; you cannot just return them. Though Jim Collins asserts that getting the wrong people out and the right people in[83] is the way to get started toward a good-to-great organization, it is not always possible. In those cases, it is the ideal time to exercise your empathy.

Terminating or transferring a difficult employee is the easy way out.[84] If you are building a team, there are always going to be conflicts. Sometimes a negative personality trait rears its ugly head in a follower, and it catches you completely by surprise. My first opportunity to mentor an employee in a civilian leadership position happened at my first health care management position.

---

[78] Peterson and Seligman 2004.
[79] Peterson and Seligman 2004.
[80] Center for Creative Leadership 2008.
[81] Senior fellow, Harvard Business School, and former chairman and CEO of Medtronic.
[82] George 2015.
[83] Collins 2001a.
[84] There are always reasons (illegal, immoral, or unethical behaviors) to terminate an employee. Here we are talking about a difficult employee.

One of my employees was an ambitious young man who seemed to rub people the wrong way. Let's call him George. I'm proud to say that George is now a leader both by position and action. Our mentor-mentee relationship started when I caught George with his feet up on his desk midday. That was an obviously unacceptable behavior given the amount of work that we were behind at the time. I saw my opportunity in a moment of clarity: I could go the disciplinary route or the mentorship route. Choosing one over the other was easy because my own mentor in the organization always told us to err on the side of compassion. I was motivated to follow his example.

I walked into the office, closing the door behind me. I started with the five whys[85] to determine the reason he wasn't contributing. George was especially well-educated and certified for his position. His talents were underutilized by the company and by the former management team. I came to the conclusion that he needed an opportunity to excel and to use the skills and abilities that we had collaboratively identified in him during our one-on-one mentoring sessions. Within the constraints of the union contract, we put George in charge of a process improvement project during the time he used to put his feet up on the desk. He excelled. George's coworkers were stunned at his transformation. His attitude and his performance were exceptional.

That seemingly simple change was an aha moment for me. A leader must *choose* to care, whether or not their followers seem to care. A leader *always* cares. I realized that a leader must always lead with individualized compassion. The natural extension of that compassionate and caring choice is to invest the time to mentor followers so that they can become leaders themselves.

Leadership interactions are further informed by any mentor a person happens to choose. Let me take a minute to emphasize the importance of choosing mentors and of choosing the right mentors for your personal and career[86] development. Mentors are crucial for leadership development.[87]

> Setting an example is not the main means of
> influencing others; it is the only means.
> —Albert Einstein

---

[85] Gemba Gembutsu, or *place* and *information* in Japanese, refers to the practice of asking *why did a failure occur* five times to come to a more complete understanding in simple root cause analysis (RCA).
[86] Zachary 2005.
[87] De Pree 1989.

MENTORSHIP INVOLVES DILIGENT WORK.

When setting out on a journey,
do not seek advice from someone who has never left home.
—Jalal al-Din Rumi [88]

Ideally, a mentor will have experience. However, experience is not the end-all and be-all. Experience is a qualification to be a subject matter expert (SME) and a prerequisite to be a trainer. Experience does not mean that a person has done the self-improvement and critical reflection necessary to have developed themselves as leaders. It does not mean that person is a leader with integrity. A mentor must behave in a manner that is internally and externally consistent.

A mentor is not simply a trainer. They are a coach, and a coach develops relationships with their team members. If you want to be a leader with integrity, then find a mentor with integrity. No one can enhance skills within you that they do not possess.

Mentoring is a brain to pick, an ear to listen,
and a push in the right direction.
—John Crosby [89]

None of us knows it all. There is nothing wrong with not knowing everything, and leveraging your mentors will provide a necessary springboard to propel you into previously out-of-reach skills and abilities.[90] Mentors should engage in scaffolding[91] with their mentees. Scaffolding is a commonplace concept in the classroom. If a student is not able to perform an academic task, often a teacher will assign another student to assist. The gap between the two students' knowledge of the subject is less than the gap between the student and teacher.

Scaffolding provides that extra support needed to reach a new level of performance. Using a mentor to *pull* you past your current capabilities shifts the zone of proximal development as learning occurs. A capable mentor will be able to identify the gaps in knowledge and assist the mentee to overcome those gaps using scaffolding.

---

[88] Thirteenth-century (1207–1273) Persian Muslim poet and Sufi mystic.
[89] American politician from the state of Massachusetts (1859–1943).
[90] Vygotsky 1978 (concept of the zone of proximal development, p. 86).
[91] Wood, Bruner, and Ross 1976.

It is not possible to have too many mentors; nor should you limit the number of people that you are willing to mentor.[92] Giving or receiving mentorship shapes not only someone else's leadership capabilities but their entire outlook on life.

The delicate balance of mentoring someone is
not creating them in your own image,
but giving them the opportunity to create themselves.
—Steven Spielberg

---

[92] Lorenz 2012.

CHAPTER RECAP

Integrity increases transparency. It is based on individual values and requires coherence between those values and leadership actions.

- Leaders must act with integrity. Always.
- Crucibles aid in the development of leadership characteristics and serve to refine a leader's commitment to acting with integrity.
- Mentors are crucial to leadership development.
- Mentors are coaches.
- Mentors scaffold leadership behaviors and practices for their mentees.

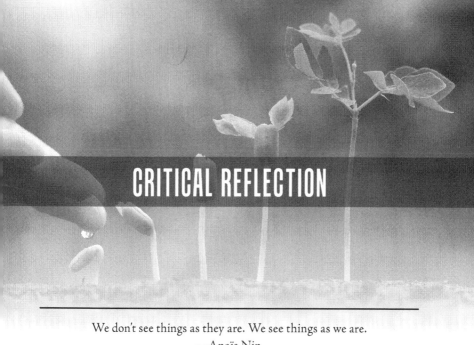

CRITICAL REFLECTION

We don't see things as they are. We see things as we are.
—Anaïs Nin

It's 1999. *The Matrix*[93] has just premiered in theaters, and I'm obsessed. The digital effects were awesome, the soundtrack was edgy, and the motif was exciting. What really caught my interest was an existential question, originally posed by Morpheus. He offers Keanu Reeves's character, Thomas Anderson/ Neo, the red pill or the blue pill. *You take the blue pill, the story ends. You wake up in your bed and believe whatever you want to believe. You take the red pill, you stay in Wonderland, and I show you how deep the rabbit hole goes.* Neo has a choice to make.

René Descartes originally described the philosophical underpinnings of being skeptical of our physical sensations in his 1641 work, *Meditations on First Philosophy*.[94] He was followed by several other influential philosophers in this vein of thought.[95] To be clear, I don't believe we exist in a computer-generated reality. However, that scene was an eye-opening realization for me. I realized that I needed to be mentally prepared to examine and potentially reject my mental preconceptions. I had to question my reality in order to learn about myself and the world that I inhabited.

My choice was the same as Neo's: (1) to continue to live a life devoid

---

[93] Wachowski and Wachowski 1999.
[94] 1979.
[95] See Peter Unger's *Evil Scientist* and Hilary Putnam's *Brain in a Vat*.

of critical reflection, the easy route, or (2) to walk the more cognitively and emotionally uncomfortable path, to choose the red pill. I was preconfigured for my journey of self-development by a blockbuster movie. Though the Wachowski brothers may have introduced the idea to my mind, the real work of critical reflection had yet to begin in me.

A loss of perspective can allow even healthy emotional responses to spiral out of control. A healthy sense of detachment, a higher mental state that allows us to passively observe and thereby regulate our emotional responses,[96] is something toward which we should daily strive as leaders.

As Miyamoto Musashi said, "If you wish to control others, you must first control yourself."[97] Developing self-control is necessary for any leader. Having self-control means that you are not subject to the whims of your emotions. Subduing emotional responses in favor of a long-term goal is willpower.[98] In order to maintain control over emotional responses, you must first hone the skill to monitor them.

As humans, we have the ability, unique in the animal kingdom, to observe our thoughts as they pass through our brains. As we monitor these thoughts, we have the additional ability to control them. This is the simple definition of metacognition.[99] Practice is required to develop the ability to self-monitor. Self-monitoring involves doing difficult mental work. That work commences with monitoring emotionally driven thoughts. Once the thoughts become distinguishable on the canvas of your mind, it is possible to determine the emotional antecedents of those thoughts. The next step is to choose and modify the thoughts. External pressures too often force reactive, emotional thoughts to the fore.

The field cannot be seen from within the field.
—Ralph Waldo Emerson

Perspective involves an awareness of self and others that can be frightening and disturbing[100] at times because awareness opens the leader to a level of empathy and vulnerability. A leader must intimately understand their motives and character. Part of gaining an understanding of self is metacognitively viewing and regulating your reactions by selecting and modifying thoughts.

---

[96] Chan 2007.
[97] Miyamoto and Harris 1974.
[98] Willpower is one of the key requirements in Jim Collins' fifth-level leader.
[99] Martinez 2006.
[100] Spears 2005.

Carefully use the emotional distance that perspective gives to practice patience and self-control. Perspective, thinking before acting, provides consistency and stability in your working environment.[101]

Your past shapes the present. It crafts the lens through which you perceive the world. Were you raised poor? Rich? Middle class? Were your parents left, middle, or center of the political spectrum? Were you raised to cherish a certain concept of morality? Were you raised in a household where education was considered important? Did your parents graduate from high school, college, graduate school? These questions may seem like nothing more than noise to some people, but that could not be further from the truth.

It requires troublesome work to undertake the alteration of old beliefs.
—John Dewey [102]

Leadership development begins with your family.[103] Understanding how your past influences your character, decision-making, and frame of reference is of critical importance to a clear understanding and regulation of self.

YOUR PAST SHAPES BUT DOES NOT PREDICT YOUR PRESENT.

Understanding, incorporating, and moving beyond some of the negative things that happened in your past can redefine your vision of the present, offering different choices and reshaping the lens through which you view your world. That understanding, incorporating, and moving on involves the practice of critical reflection.

Critical reflection takes each of these and many more questions and closely analyzes the impact that they have on your psyche and, by extension, on your fitness to lead. You will find that unresolved emotional issues will absolutely lead to leadership pitfalls. The Dalai Lama exhorts us to seek critical philosophical inquiry and ethical living with contemplative practice.[104] Critical reflection is a contemplative practice that incorporates philosophical inquiry. One of the benefits of critical reflection is that you will become more conscious and intentional about your leadership practice.

---

[101] Headquarters, United States Army, 2006.
[102] John Dewey (1859–1952) was one of the founders of the philosophical school of pragmatism and was a pioneer in functional psychology and educational reform.
[103] Zaleznik 1992.
[104] Bstan-'dzin-rgya-mtsho 2011.

Once you have incorporated this new understanding into your practice, take a step back. How might your former perspective have limited you in the past? What of your upbringing do you need to carry forward with you because it is valuable? What should you discard or modify? These are all questions that should be answered in order to fully realize the holistic approach to Living Your Leadership. You should be able to identify and fully understand where your perspective comes from so that you can modify perceptions at will.

Even if you go through the activity above initially, it is something that you will have to do multiple times throughout your leadership journey. Novel situations will arise. Situations that will trigger emotions from your past. Those emotions will have to be critically reexamined in order to fully incorporate the emotion around your experience into authentic self-knowledge. You must reconcile the emotions and reactions within yourself when you consider new stimuli as well. Develop the self-control to cultivate a useful perspective. Your new perspective is grounded in past experience, since your view of the present is shaped by your memory of the past. The practice of self-control in critical reflection allows you to incorporate emotions, perceptions, and stimuli in the most ethical and thoughtful way.

It is not only possible but necessary to realize that one can take offense to something but not be offended by it. This is an incredibly difficult thing to do, but the practice of self-control and the development of a healthy self-perception demand the ability.

As the manager for biomedical engineering at a hospital in the Silicon Valley, I had ultimate accountability for a portfolio of strategic service delivery, educational, and budgetary initiatives in the service area. With responsibility for thousands of medical devices in the hospital, I was bound to encounter an array of negative and positive customer service interactions, despite the professionalism expected in a health care setting.

I had been in the position for some months when my first real customer blowup happened. Evidently, there was a shortage of a particular expensive medical device in a unit, and the manager of that unit needed someone to take their frustration out on. I had learned during my time in Iraq that taking a breath and evaluating a situation before responding was advisable, so I put that into practice as I stood in the hallway being berated by this person. They contended that my department was ineffective, that I was underqualified, and that it was all my fault.

It would have been easy to take offense and snap back. As a leader in the hospital, I knew that my role was to support patient care, and my duties to the inpatient units were clearly defined in the service level agreement. This person was lashing out because they were emotionally immature, not because I had done anything deserving of a dressing down. By weathering his verbal storm and offering to help him find a solution, I built a bridge where there had previously only been a wall.

Something *can* be offensive, objectively speaking. There are certain things that are morally and ethically deplorable that should offend our sensibilities. The distinction must be drawn, however, between something being offensive and our being offended by it. As a self-aware and self-confident leader, you should possess the moral objectivity and perspective to be able to isolate and examine your emotional reaction to an objectionable situation. You should employ your hard-won self-control to view the potentially upsetting scenario and respond to it in a professionally unemotional and appropriate way.

We all run into situations where someone accosts us with an outburst that seems exaggerated beyond all reason. As a leader, *regulating* your response to that overemotional outburst is an aspect of emotional intelligence.[105] Determining the cause of the outburst involves empathy, while not taking immediate offense requires active humility and self-control. Self-regulation is an EQ-related trait that needs to be exercised by leaders[106] in difficult situations so that they do not simply allow their brain-to-speech filter to spew whatever they are thinking.

LEADERS DO NOT HAVE THE LUXURY OF BEING OFFENDED.

Offense is taken because leaders fail to understand that most things are not about them; criticism is often just someone venting. Developing a humble, empathetic mind-set and responding through self-regulation does not happen overnight. It takes practice and internal work to develop self-control.

> Choose not to be harmed—and you won't feel harmed.
> Don't feel harmed—and you haven't been.
> —Marcus Aurelius

More on the subject of objectivity: perspective and objectivity should not be used interchangeably. This is more than a simple semantic difference, in that objectivity implies your emotions have been disconnected from the subject. While this is appropriate in some circumstances, it is not appropriate when dealing with the human side of leadership.

---

[105] Figure 4.
[106] George 2015.

In contrast to objectivity, perspective is a mental exercise that provides distance between an event and its emotional impact. Perspective allows incorporation of the experience into our mental models so that it can be analyzed and learned from. Perspective does not detach emotional consequence; rather, it tempers our reactions.

Most decisions affect your followers in one way or another. The intrinsic value of humanity and the recognition that you exist to serve your followers should supersede your desire to be objective in your decision-making processes.

> Self-reverence, self-knowledge, self-control.
> These three alone lead one to sovereign power.
> —Lord Tennyson[107]

Certain business considerations have to take precedence,[108] but the human factor should never be overlooked. That is why it is appropriate to use the word perspective instead of objectivity when describing how to make decisions as a leader. The use of *perspective* when making leadership decisions allows you to remove the immediacy of the negative emotional response. Taking a step back, metaphorically speaking, means that the leader retains useful emotions when dealing with the care of followers, emotions like pity and love.

Among the other things that he was famous for, Marcus Aurelius was one of the great stoic thinkers of his day. His fame spread as he pursued the German campaigns in the later Roman Empire. He was perceived by many as one of the Five Great Emperors of Rome[109] and was also famous in philosophical circles. One of the practices that Marcus Aurelius swore by is taking a few moments at the end of each day in contemplation. During those few minutes, he would critically reflect on his actions and their impacts, contemplating the future.

Our lives are composed of decisions. Realizing that the color of your thoughts shapes the day that you're going to have makes the idea of meditating on those thoughts more palatable, even desirable. Your thoughts impact the relationship you have with those around you. Meditation is a deliberate act that primes the mind, allowing you to critically assess your thoughts and feelings through focused relaxation.

---

[107] Alfred Tennyson (1809–1892) was poet laureate of Great Britain and Ireland during the Victorian era.

[108] That is, legal and contractual concerns.

[109] The five emperors in unbroken (not blood) succession were Nerva, Trajan, Hadrian, Antoninus Pius, and Marcus Aurelius.

You need to avoid certain things in your train of thought: Everything random, everything irrelevant. And certainly, everything self-important or malicious. You need to get used to winnowing your thoughts, so that if someone says, "What are you thinking about?" you can respond at once (and truthfully) that you are thinking this or thinking that.

—Marcus Aurelius

Meditation is often seen in some conservative Western societies as inadvisable or incompatible with Judeo-Christian values, but this could not be further from the truth. The profound rest you can achieve during meditation results in a needed refreshment of mental and emotional resources,[110] not to mention that it is easier to examine the world and your place in it while outward distractions are minimized.

We must be silent before we can listen.
We must listen before we can learn.
We must learn before we can prepare.
We must prepare before we can serve.
We must serve before we can lead.
—William Arthur Ward [111]

There are several recommended ways to start a meditation session. One of the first things to do is to clear the physical area around you if at all possible. Chaos on the outside can negatively impact the mental stillness that you are trying to achieve. Disarray in your surroundings can be echoed by disarray in your thinking; your outer circumstances can be a mirror for your inner mental state.

You should also remain still. Sitting in repose will allow you to most effectively clear your mind because you are not using muscles in your body that could be otherwise used in productive activity. You do not have to feel as connected to the world around you if you are not moving around in your physical space. When I meditate, either in prayer or in thoughtful reflective practice, I like to close the door to my office, dim the lights, and turn on a fan to dull my auditory sense with white noise.

Lieutenant Barker was miserable. He'd been disciplined for being late, had missed questions on his monthly classified missile test, and worst of all,

---

[110] Cashman 2008.
[111] Quoted in Leadership with a Human Touch (June 1, 1999, p. 11).

he had been separated from his wife despite assurances that they would be stationed together. Barker was one of my subordinate officers. He was a good guy, young and intelligent with a facility for making others feel welcome. His test scores and behavior weren't indicative of the type of officer that he could be. I had been tasked with writing the paperwork that would ruin his career.

It wasn't a task that I wanted to do. The hesitation was grounded in more than just my preference for education and training than punishment; the situation felt wrong. As I walked into the headquarters building from the frigid North Dakota winter, I knocked the snow off my boots and entered my office, fully intending to do as I had been instructed. I shut the door, shucked my parka with frustration, and tossed my gloves into the corner of the room. As I sat there, staring at the computer screen, I breathed slowly in and out, taking the time to calm myself.

I was Lt. Barker's boss. What were my responsibilities as his leader? His mentor? I hadn't taken the time yet to talk to him, to ask him about his troubles. As I sat in my quiet office, I formed a plan. I took the time and developed the perspective to see Lt. Barker as a person. He was struggling and needed guidance. Though he didn't remain an active-duty member of the air force, Barker's time at Minot became much more bearable. We developed a close relationship and went on dozens of alerts together. It was that meditative time that allowed me the mental reorientation necessary to make the leaderly decision.

Meditative practice is enhanced by dulling our sensory perceptions. Consider lowering the lights or closing your eyes. The eyes are our primary means of information gathering about the world. They can distract your inner calm by attempting to process visual stimuli during your attempt at relaxation. Meditation will encourage you to cultivate, appreciate, and use mental solitude to benefit your spiritual, emotional, and physical well-being.

> There is no need to go to India to find peace.
> You will find that deep place of silence right in your
> room, your garden or even your bathtub.
> —Dr. Elisabeth Kübler-Ross

The next step is to relax. Relaxation is not a physical or mental process, per se. If it helps you to think of it that way, then I would encourage you to do so. Ideally, you should be able to simply let go. You should sit and detach cognitively from the world around you—to surrender. This cognitive detachment does not mean that you are no longer thinking. Rather, you will be attentive to the world around you in a different way. A mindful reflection is what you hope to attain when you relax in this manner.

There are many books about meditation and relaxation techniques, but this is not one of them. My hope is that this brief overview gives you a quick dip of the toe into the still waters of meditation. To reap the greatest benefit from practicing critical self-reflection, it should be performed in a relaxed mental state.

You will find that once you can achieve a practice of mindfulness, present-state awareness, you will have greater control over your attention. And by attention, I mean that you will be able to control what you will and will not spend your time thinking about[112] and ultimately have a higher level of control over your mental and emotional state. With the practice of mindfulness, you will find that actions flow more authentically from a grounded place of repose.

This meditative practice lies in opposition to automatic, knee-jerk responses to external stimuli.[113] Those reactions are to be avoided at all costs because without knowledge of what is motivating your emotions or actions, you lose control of your reactions and cannot authentically lead others. A certain level of self-awareness, self-acceptance, and self-control are necessary at all times.

TO WHAT SHOULD WE DEVOTE OUR ATTENTION?

It seems that every day we are inundated with ideas, images, and sound bites. We live in a world that expresses itself 140 characters at a time, all the time, day and night. These stimuli root in our skulls. With the sheer amount of information available to us, it is extremely difficult for us to focus our attention on what is important, that which adds value to our lives.

Critical reflection and meditation are two ways that will encourage your brain to understand what is value added. They will allow you to direct your attention to those things that are meaningful and impactful. Meaningful experiences and cogent thoughts should be critically analyzed and processed.

Rather than automatically reacting to anything that occurs to you externally, your practice should slowly mature into the ability to step outside yourself. You should be able to allow those experiences and stimuli to pass in front of your critical mind's eye so that you can choose what to react to.

---

[112] Posner and Boies 1971.
[113] Bryant and Kazan 2013, p. 51–52.

This practice requires a great deal of control and patience. Critical reflection, questioning ordinary external stimuli, is not common.

It is far more common for people to automatically, almost subconsciously, process and react in preconfigured ways. Past experiences have informed our minds to respond in templated ways. These schema,[114] templates, or scripts that allow us to more quickly and effectively respond to outside stimuli must be analyzed and questioned. Even though a situation might look similar to a past situation, that does not necessarily mean it needs to be reacted to in the same way—or even reacted to at all.

In general, we spend far too little time examining what we consume experientially, and not enough time examining the process by which it percolates into our mind. We seldom even consider the reactions we have to our experiences. Understanding our own mental processes allows us to have a firmer grip on our emotional reactions. Control is eminently desirable in that it leads to a high level of rationality and self-control.

> The ability to subordinate an impulse to a value
> is the essence of the proactive person.
> —Stephen Covey

Self-control is achieved once we can more closely regulate what enters our consciousness rather than simply absorbing it. With that regulation comes a better understanding of our values and a firmer knowledge of what is likely to motivate us as leaders. Regulation implies the ability to process external stimuli, questioning it against previously held beliefs and self-knowledge. Using the techniques described above, those experiences should then deliberately be incorporated, discarded, or modified.

An added benefit to self-knowledge and control in mindfulness practice is that it opens us up to a better understanding of others. Control over our thought processes allows us to identify a lack of control in others. Identifying weakness in others does not grant the leader license to condescend. Observing weakness in others with a caring heart allows you to embrace a greater degree of empathy.

Empathy will be discussed in a later chapter; however, one of the important aspects of mindfulness, of observing and regulating our own thoughts, is to cultivate a practice of nonjudgment. Refusing to judge and condemn is part of

---

[114] The study of schemas as templates for understanding behavior, contradictory to the popular study of behaviorism at the time, was initiated by Frederic Bartlett in the early 1930s.

the self-control. Knowing that you have advanced in a fashion that is superior to another does not mean that you are, in fact, superior to another. Appreciating the inherent dignity of humanity and practicing humility means that you understand at a deep level that self-improvement can be meaningful only if it is used to lift others.

Any critical reflection of self should involve the definition of the self. What do we mean by *I*? A possible definition is that entity that detachedly examines your thoughts as they pass through your mind. Still others describe *I* as a collection of successive perceptions, a bundle of perceptions, like humanist David Hume.[115] "When I enter most intimately into what I call myself I always stumble on some particular perception or other ... and never can observe anything but the perception."[116] For the purposes of this text and critical self-reflection, *I* will be defined as the Ego, that part of ourselves that is eminently in our control to modify at will.

Let us take a moment to discuss a piece of the lexicon for this book that could be confusing. One of the words in this book that has a dual meaning, which I hope not to use inappropriately, is ego. The Ego, the proper noun (in the Jungian and Freudian sense), refers to the mental or inner self. However, in this book, *egotism* or *ego*, the common noun, refers to an inflated or selfish sense of self.

Though egotism is not a desirable leadership characteristic, I do not mean to imply that ego is unacceptable. At its most basic level, a healthy ego is the result of natural mental development. In fact, having a robust sense of self allows us to develop self-confidence and esteem. As social animals, a limited amount of ego allows us to be evolutionarily competitive with one another. As the Dalai Lama states, however, once egoism reaches the point where you start to disregard the good of others in favor of your own interests, that is where the line is drawn between healthy and unhealthy ego.[117]

Part of achieving self-actualization is the realization that you are not the most important thing. Developing yourself is necessary, but without the effort of community, it is unlikely that the journey to self-actualization will ever be fully realized. Serving others means that they will have the benefit of your help on their own path. This reciprocal relationship is the bedrock of community. In order to focus beyond individual needs and concerns, a leader must stop worrying about themselves to the exclusion of others.[118] The subordination

---

[115] Hume 2000.
[116] Treatise, 1.4.6. para. 3.
[117] Bstan-'dzin-rgya-mtsho 2011.
[118] Hayward 2007.

of your ego to the needs of others is a crucial step in the journey toward self-actualization.

One of the reasons it is so hard to understand oneself, to achieve self-mastery, is that a person is *more* than just the accumulation of experiences. It is narrow-minded to take a snapshot in time and define a person based on that solitary picture. People have the ability to choose, to think about thinking, to plan their actions, or to allow instinct to have control. People grow and change.

In any case, the environmental and social factors that play a part in a person's life, their emotions, and their experience-based schema all contribute to the choices a person will make. A person is acting out Living Their Leadership if their choices are based on predetermined priorities and values while taking into consideration a thorough knowledge of self. Concurrently, a leader must not neglect the needs and concerns of others.

Thinking of life as a race is a typically Western idea. Saint Paul says, "Do you not know that in a race all the runners run, but only one gets the prize? Run in such a way as to get the prize."[119] St. Paul is speaking metaphorically about the way to live a life that will lead to rewards in heaven, but the metaphorical meaning that many people choose to see is that winning is the important thing.

Living Your Leadership is a journey, a distance race that "is about training and being prepared for opportunities when they come—you don't train for a marathon in the same way you train for a 50-yard dash!"[120] The process of human development is a lifelong effort.[121] It is easy to picture a swift footrace of several hundred meters when *winning a race* is mentioned, but like so many metaphors, our first impression of it falls woefully short of its true meaning. There was a deeper and richer significance to being a follower (runner) of Christ in the life of St. Paul. His daily acts of grit and perseverance, of charity and love, were monumental and resource intensive.

St. Paul worked. Every day, he understood himself and his mission better than the day before. As he worked (raced), his struggles shaped his psyche. The world he lived in was incredibly harsh by modern standards. St. Paul didn't run his race wearing high-tech, gold Nike running shoes on a rubberized track with a Gatorade stand at the finish. He also wasn't wearing an Armani suit, sporting a Rolex, or strutting around in highly polished Salvatore Ferragamo shoes while rushing to an executive stakeholder meeting in his many-windowed high-rise office building. Paul wore sandals in the desert. His occupation for some time was *tentmaker*. He used the money he made to support his mission

---

[119] 1 Corinthians 9:24 NIV.

[120] Lorenz 2012, p. 12.

[121] Baltes and Reese 1984.

of preaching the good news. He served the poor and infirm, knowing his most likely earthly outcome was a martyr's death. It is a bleak picture of the finish line of his earthly race, isn't it? That is why equating a quick race with the defeat of other runners is shortsighted.

St. Paul, like all of us, was running a distance race. We pause to help those along the way. We show respect, mercy, sportsmanship, and kindness to other runners. We sacrifice our petty needs for others as we lead the way. We push through our pain and celebrate successes. It doesn't matter where you are in your personal journey; your life will not start when you reach some arbitrary finish line.[122]

Sitting with your thoughts. One of the more difficult practices the leader has is being able to sit with their thoughts. It can sometimes seem like a maelstrom venturing into your workplace. You take requests, hear complaints, strategize, and perform daily tasks. Oftentimes, one of the solutions to this problem is attempting to give immediate answers and solutions to any problems that crop up.

IMMEDIATE SOLUTIONS SHOULD BE AVOIDED AT ALL COSTS.

When a situation arises that requires some strategic thought, the leader should take the time necessary to review that thought in their own mind. This is almost universally applicable to any major decision that person has to make. A leader should always have at least one contingency in mind, but even the best strategic thinkers among us are not able to immediately come up with tertiary stratagems at a moment's notice. Indeed, it will make you feel vulnerable to sit with your thoughts and give them the time that they need to properly percolate in your mind. Being at ease with feelings of vulnerability is a strength in leaders.

The fallacy of the immediate decision is something that I often see in new leaders. They feel like their job is to get out in front and start making decisions. Except in cases of life-or-death immediacy, there is nearly always time to take a breath and consider decisions critically. The more seasoned leaders typically take the time to suss out various second-order effects of the decisions that they plan to make. They pause to validate that those decisions are in alignment with the strategic mission, vision, and values of the organization.

---

[122] Sinek 2011.

We can make, to ourselves, very much stronger suggestions
than anyone else can, whoever that person may be.
—Émile Coué de la Châtaigneraie[123]

The bedrock of interpersonal skill is self-knowledge. Achieving a solid understanding of self—strengths, weaknesses, and personality—is required before effective communication can occur. This is harder than its sounds. The goal is to fine-tune self-knowledge while helping others move forward. A good way to determine whether you understand yourself in a practical way is to practice asking yourself behavioral interview questions.

A simple internet search will yield some excellent behavioral interview questions. Behavioral interview questions involve scenarios that will yield concrete examples of how you have reacted in real-world situations. For example:

- Give me an example of a time that you worked well under pressure.
- Tell me about how you work with others.
    - o   Do you take the lead in team scenarios? Why? Why not?
- What does being a leader mean to you?
    - o   What skills do you have that make you a good leader?
    - o   What skills do you have that make you a good follower?
- How do you handle mistakes at work?
    - o   Tell me about a situation where that happened.
- Recall a time you disagreed with a superior.
    - o   How did you handle it?
- How would you describe your strengths and weaknesses while working on a team?
- Give an example of how your strengths and weaknesses have played out in your past experience.

How does one become more self-aware? It is a lifelong effort, though it can be accelerated by critical self-reflection (discernment) and focused intellectual effort. Some people are naturally more self-aware than others. Valuing objective dialogue about strengths and weaknesses within a family unit, effective mentorship, or an introspective disposition can provide a boost to self-awareness. Consequently, working in those directions will increase your self-awareness, and self-leadership emerges from self-awareness.[124]

---

[123] French psychologist and pharmacist (1857–1926) who developed the psychotherapeutic method of conscious autosuggestion.
[124] Bryant and Kazan 2013, p. 13.

CHAPTER RECAP

Critical reflection is a self-reflective skill that encourages perspective, leads to better decision-making, and reduces cognitive bias.

- Perspective is not the same as objectivity. Perspective is gained through experience and reflection.
- An understanding and acceptance of your past leads to the positive integration of values and experiences that give shape to the lens with which you perceive the world.
- Do not let the criticism of others detract from your self-worth or dictate your actions.
- Consider meditation to increase focus and mindfulness.
- Grow beyond thinking of yourself.
- Self-actualization results in empathy and compassion as the attention shifts to others.

OPTIMISM AND GRATITUDE

Perpetual optimism is a force multiplier.
—General Colin Powell, United States Army

I was always interested in the mission of the ICBM fleet. Strategic deterrence made sense to me. During the evening and early-morning hours, while there was little to occupy my time on alert, I would sit and read the technical orders and manuals so I could better understand the weapon system. One of my goals while in ICBM operations was to be nominated and sent on a *Glory Trip* to test launch the Minuteman III. These tests happened roughly three times a year in order to validate the effectiveness, readiness, and accuracy of the weapon system. I wanted to be part of the crew to actually turn the launch key and watch the trail of fire as it ascended into the atmosphere.

I got my chance. Six crewmembers traveled from North Dakota to California's lush Central Coast in February 2007. My crew partner and I were the ones to provide the final key turn that sent the unarmed Minuteman III intercontinental ballistic missile into the sky. The test flight was code-named *Glory Trip 193GM*. The unarmed reentry vehicle reentered the atmosphere on a ballistic trajectory to a predetermined target in the Marshall Islands. It was one of the most unique and exciting experiences I participated in while I served.

My selection to the test launch team was more than just a reward for my performance during my crew time. During the trip, I had the opportunity to learn from engineers and specialists about the missile, its fuel, its internal structure, the launch configuration, and how it appears on the weapons system display console. Gaining that deeper understanding, coupled with my internal desire to do more and serve better, solidified the congruence of my personal goals with an extrinsic motivator. The extrinsic tool was my selection to participate in the test launch, and the alignment of my goal to enhance my weapons system knowledge pushed my locus of causality completely internal.[125] I had an inherent satisfaction with my job that I had not experienced prior to the trip.

One of the more neglected areas of personal and professional development is focusing on moving motivation, our passion to achieve, from an external to an internal focus. Our natural inclination to be motivated toward a certain activity is central to our social, cognitive, and physical development.[126] Without the natural drive to pursue our inherent interests, it is unlikely that anyone would bother developing themselves.

> Virtually nothing on earth can stop a person with a
> positive attitude who has his goal clearly in sight.
> —Denis Waitley

Leadership is challenging[127] and, at times, demoralizing and difficult. It, like everything else in life, is harder if you whine about it. Complaining, even if it is just in your mind, is poisonous. Internally, it casts a pall over your view of the world. People are unlikely to be inspired to follow a downcast leader. Externally, if you complain about your duty as a leader, you let your followers know that you cannot be trusted with their well-being. How would you feel as a follower if your leader complained about their tasks? Complaining erodes trust and faith in your leadership.

> Cheerfulness prepares a glorious mind for all the noblest acts.
> —St. Elizabeth Ann Seton

Dale Carnegie[128] wrote my personal favorite leadership self-help book: *How to Win Friends and Influence People*. In it, he talks about a dog, the animal that is always happy to see you, who has a perpetual smile, who wags his tail and makes the world a happier place. Though taking lessons from a pet might seem like an oversimplification, try it out sometime and measure the results

---

[125] See figure 8.
[126] Ryan and Deci 2000.
[127] Lorenz 2012.
[128] Carnegie 1998.

by the number of positive interactions you have in your office. When you greet someone with a smile, they will probably smile back.

I learned from Dale Carnegie and from practice that smiles are infectious, and so are frowns. Leaders convey *enthusiasm* and *optimism*.[129] A leader who comes to work happy and excited to tackle the challenges of the day will inspire and motivate their followers to achieve.[130]

Metaphors like the grateful puppy tend to break down. They are useful tools to get your message across, but if they are stretched too far, they become cumbersome or unrealistic. The happy dog does not understand the difference between realistic and unrealistic optimism. A dog is pretty happy almost all the time!

ONLY A FOOL WALKS AROUND WITH A SMILE PLASTERED ON THEIR FACE ALL THE TIME.

With all of life's various challenges, its ups and downs, gravitas is sometimes required in place of mindless optimism. Realistic optimism involves the acceptance that good and bad things happen, but there is an opportunity to make *good* regardless of the circumstances.[131] The leadership behaviors that you demonstrate will be your legacy. What legacy would you prefer to leave in your workplace?

I always like to look on the optimistic side of life.
—Walt Disney

Having an attitude of gratitude is useless without corresponding action.

The question that should accost you daily is, How do you put your gratitude into practice? Accosting is meant to be an uncomfortable term. Being accosted by gratitude, by humility, and by selflessness means that you are caught unawares, that you are forced to come face-to-face with an idea that you had not been prepared for.

Brené Brown, in her series of talks about the power of vulnerability, compares having and wearing yoga clothing to being asked to perform yoga. Her engaging oratory style imparts humor to the comparison. She draws

---

[129] Maister 2014.
[130] Cockerell 2008.
[131] Bryant and Kazan 2013, p. 23.

attention to how commonplace the misunderstanding of the importance of practicing gratitude is for mental health and happiness in our daily lives. I don't mean to say that an *attitude of gratitude* is not a positive mental state or something that shouldn't be aspired to. Getting to a place where you can genuinely feel an *attitude of gratitude* requires work to achieve. The rather pithy Hallmark greeting card idea of gratitude cheapens the deep and meaningful emotion and actions that underscore the importance of gratitude in our daily lives.

Service is a meaningful opportunity to live gratitude. In a business setting, a leader needs to give appreciation to employees who are having a difficult time. A leader can turn around employees who are failing to meet goals, that are having interpersonal issues, or that seem to be contrarian for no good reason. Gratitude confers esteem on others. True gratitude implies humility, self-knowledge, and service. It requires that a leader understand the intrinsic value of others, rather than just how their work serves the organization.[132]

Being thankful for that work is useful only inasmuch as you communicate it to the employee. Express genuine gratitude by recognizing them in front of others. An employee will be more motivated receiving positive feedback based not only on routine performance but on extraordinary achievements. Meaningful, positive performance feedback enhances intrinsic motivation[133] and is the basis of a positive, autonomy-supporting work environment.[134]

It is easy to get stuck in a tree full of monkeys when you are at work. Envision the tree as a hierarchy. The lowest level of the tree is full of the frontline employees. The next level is frontline management, then middle management, executives, and so on. A dictatorial leader makes sure that everyone at the top of the tree looking down sees only smiles. Those miserable monkeys near the bottom looking up see only asses.[135] Every monkey deserves to have their day in the sun. If you have gotten to the point where you are a monkey in a tree, you have failed to understand and practice gratitude.

Take the time to take a step back and reflect. Recognize that the employees you have hired and trained are your most important assets. Without them, you would not be in the leadership role you enjoy. Be actively grateful for their work and for them as individuals. If you embody that perspective, your actions will be inspired by the positive outlook you have trained yourself to experience.

As a nuclear missile combat crew commander, operational knowledge

---

[132] That is, your power, ego, and reputation.
[133] Deci 1971.
[134] Vadell and Ewing 2011.
[135] Sinek 2011.

is constantly tested. In the nuclear field, there is no room for incomplete knowledge or substandard performance.[136] Regardless of the passing score of 90 percent on monthly tests, there was an implicit standard of perfection. Any missed questions on critical questions could mean the loss of countless lives if applied in a real-world operational scenario. One of the knowledge areas missileers are tested on is weapon system safety rules (WSSRs). WSSRs serve to validate that each nuclear operator knows how to launch or safe nuclear weapons.

One month, on a routine recurring test, an operator missed one of the questions. He shrugged it off, since missing only one still allowed for a passing grade. The next day, the member was called into the unit commander's office to answer for the missed question. The member explained that a passing grade was achieved, so all was well. The commander quickly corrected the member. He asked, "What part of nuclear knowledge, particularly safety-related knowledge, don't you need to know?" As it turns out, the question missed was about the safing of the weapons. If the safing procedure was performed improperly, it could result in an inadvertent nuclear missile launch.

The commander insisted that the entire unit be retrained on WSSRs. That disciplinary measure was necessary to reinforce the necessity of weapon's safety rules and testing competence. It provided a lesson after failure. The emotional struggle that the operator had to endure should have forced self-reflection, given him a chance to learn from failure, and acted as a catalyst to move motivation toward integration and identification.[137] Had the operator been more internally motivated to understand the material and dedicate himself to excellence, the need for retesting and training would have been nullified.

---

[136] Saying from Lt. Colonel Timothy Murtha, 741st Missile Squadron Director of Operations, on or around 2006. Later officially adopted by the 91st Space Wing.

[137] Figure 9.

CHAPTER RECAP

Part of being the kind of leader that people want to follow is being an unstoppable force of will and optimism.

- Cultivate realistic optimism.
- Practice gratitude until it becomes a mind-set.
- Appreciate the people you lead and show them that you do in tangible ways.

LEADING WITH HUMILITY

Remain humble, remain simple.
The more you are so, the more good you will do.
—Saint John Vianney

Code change time had come again. Code change in the ICBM community meant that two crews, four total missileers, were required to spend five days on alert in the missile field. It is one of the most stressful and technically demanding operations we conduct during the course of the year. The crews are required not only to swap the codes used in the LCC, but they are required to coordinate with the maintenance and security teams out in the field performing the complementary code swap-outs at the ICBMs themselves.

These complementary code components comprise the system that ensures command and control, the ability to launch or inhibit the launch of the nuclear weapons. There are hundreds of documented actions and phone calls in that narrow space of time that the crews are responsible for. Pieces of the launch console are physically removed and replaced during the operation. There are many technical orders and instructions that must be followed perfectly during code change, including the unclassified AFI 91-114.

> 9.1. Do not let an individual, a code courier team, or an installation team handle, have access to, or have any combination of codes or encoder or decoder devices, at the same time that reveals the information needed to enable

or launch a nuclear weapon. A Two-Person Concept team must control any device containing operational code data until the data is overwritten, superseded, or destroyed. (AFI 91-114[138])

Our best crew commanders were scheduled as primary, daytime crew for the code change each year. There were enough individuals to have taken the code change duty without touching some of the primarily command-level, training, or evaluation crews. Each year, there were several of those officers who would volunteer for the duty out of an obligation they felt to train the next generation of missileers.

This was a big sacrifice for these members and their families. While five days doesn't sound particularly onerous, the level of scrutiny that they have to endure, coupled with the amount of time in preparation and on site, made for a challenging week. In addition, these senior-level individuals were committed, based on their positions, to a mostly Monday-to-Friday work week. While they still pulled alert, they were more likely to be found in an office, teaching, evaluating, building tests or simulation scenarios, or performing the routine management side of the ICBM business.

I always admired the folks who volunteered for code change when they didn't have to. I managed to be involved in a code change each year I was on crew, despite my position as flight commander during my last code change. Having the humility to happily work side by side and train our youngest up-and-coming missileers was something that the best leaders in the ICBM community did routinely. It was always evident which of those leaders were not interested in taking code change because they felt entitled; they were too important to perform this annoying *crew dog*[139] task.

While Living Your Leadership, recognize that humility is foundational to leadership practice. Humility is closely related to the practice of self-sacrifice since, as a humble leader, you are willing to make sacrifices for those you serve. Humility recognizes that none of us are perfect.

> One thing is certain in business.
> You and everyone around you will make mistakes.
> —Richard Branson

---

[138] 2015, p. 6.

[139] Crew dog refers to missileers (like me) who were not accepted into the evaluator or instructor squadrons.

You will make mistakes. There will be times you do not know what to do. This is normal. Embrace the vulnerability that inspires in you. It will allow you to authentically lead your followers versus stomping on them. Similarly, it is normal not to know everything. It is not necessary for you to devalue yourself or your contributions in order to be humble; rather, humility recognizes that leadership success depends greatly on the success of others.

Humility involves being accountable to others, listening, and being other-centered to the point of personal sacrifice.[140] Humility is not self-effacement. Humility hinges on accurate self-appraisal. A humble leader freely gives affirmations without expecting any in return. A humble leader critically examines how they are perceived by others.

How do others see the leader? As a leader better understands the perceptions of others, they become more socially aware. This perceptive ability is like a mirror. A self-aware leader will seek to align the perception of themselves to who they authentically are. Changing behavior to align values with perception is the opposite of play acting or putting on a false front.

> Everything will line up perfectly when knowing and living
> the truth becomes more important than looking good.
> —Alan Cohen[141]

The feedback a leader gets from that mirror should be incorporated into their self-concept. Truly humble leaders value feedback from others to the point where they will seek it out on a consistent basis. Humble leaders are lifelong learners. They do not deceive themselves by thinking they are all-knowing or that there is nothing left to learn about themselves. Intellectual honesty is a hallmark of the humble leader.

> Leadership cannot exist without Humility.
> This single trait opens the leader to learning, trust, and engagement,
> which represent the foundation of all great achievements.
> —Cameron Morrissey[142]

---

[140] Poon 2006.
[141] Prolific American author and internationally recognized speaker.
[142] Best-selling author and management thought leader.

Genuine humility will be recognized by your followers. Especially in our selfie culture[143] with the pervasiveness of instant gratification, often incoherent attempts at individualism, genuineness, and humility can be difficult concepts for some people to comprehend. It is culturally understood that the way to get ahead is to project excessive self-confidence, to be the outstanding, charismatic leader. Those at the forefront of the pantheon of American leaders are larger than life and are rarely known for their humility and other-centeredness.[144] This is a generalization and is certainly not intended to imply that any culture is more or less able to produce leaders that follow the paradigm outlined in this book.

> The rare people who do become truly exceptional at something do so not because they believe they're exceptional. On the contrary, they become amazing because they're obsessed with improvement. And that obsession with improvement stems from an unerring belief that they are, in fact, not that great at all. It's anti-entitlement. People who become great at something become great because they understand that they're not already great—they are mediocre, they are average—and that they could be so much better. (Mark Manson[145])

How does a leader know that they are being ego driven rather than humble? There are several indications to be on the lookout for. When talking to followers, a leader should not be focused on what they want to get out of the conversation. They should not hold in their mind what they want to say. A humble leader makes the conscious decision to listen for understanding, not in order to respond.

> When people talk, listen completely.
> —Ernest Hemingway

> Most people do not listen with the intent to understand;
> they listen with the intent to reply.
> —Stephen Covey

---

[143] Meant broadly as digital narcissism; the obsessive need to compete by constantly posting enviable, exciting, or scandalous pictures on social media.
[144] Though that is not always the case, as with leaders like Harry Truman or George Washington and more.
[145] 2016, p. 61.

Listening is one of the most important skills a leader can develop. Followers have things that they say and things that they *mean to say* when they speak to you.[146] Watch for body language cues and be mindful of the environment so that you can most effectively understand. Engage in active listening; summarize what you heard and ask open-ended follow-up questions like, "Here is what I heard you say" and "Please, tell me more." Active listening allows for the generation of ideas, the empowerment of followers, and the development of an inclusive atmosphere in an organization.

"I carry this card with me at all times," he said, "to remind me about the most important attribute of a leader." The card reads:

**When is the last time you allowed a subordinate
to change your mind about something?**

"I want you to remember this as you leave here today and
rejoin the regular Army: Be a good listener."[147]
—General Glenn K Otis [148]

Do you feel that you are in competition with others? You should not. You are a leader, self-aware and grounded. The aspirations and successes of others should not make you fearful; rather, you should celebrate their successes. Seeking to compete with others, even if it is only in your mind, means that you feel you are not good enough. If that is the case, it is time to reflect on your value system. How are you measuring your success toward embodying the values you hold dear?

If your metric for success is a comparison to others, you have chosen an unhealthy way to measure the attainment of your goals.

Don't undermine your worth by comparing yourself with others.
It is because we are different that each of us is special.
Don't set your goals by what other people deem important.
Only you know what is best for you.
—Brian G. Dyson[149]

---

[146] Cockerell 2008.
[147] Dempsey 2017.
[148] Glenn Kay Otis (1929–2013), US Army four-star general. Quote from speech at midcareer school graduation, Fort Leavenworth, Kansas.
[149] President and CEO of Coca-Cola Enterprises. From his speech at Georgia Tech's 172nd Commencement Address, 9/6/1996.

As I was researching the subject of feedback, I encountered an interesting perspective from Kim Scott, former director at Google, faculty member at Apple University, and a CEO coach in Silicon Valley. Her impactful book, *Radical Candor*, is an eye-opening narrative. One of the most impactful takeaways that relates to Living Your Leadership is the understanding that *feedback* is annoying, but candid *guidance* is something we continuously strive to give, receive, and encourage.[150]

If you feel attacked or derided when receiving guidance, then you are experiencing an excess of ego. A humble, self-aware leader knows that most feedback is not a personal attack. Most feedback is nothing more than guidance. Whether we refer to it as feedback or guidance, it is a gift. Always seek to give and invite constructive guidance. There is a natural urge to protect oneself from difficult facts and negative feedback; that is self-importance speaking.

Humility and tenderness are not virtues of the weak, but of the strong.
—Pope Francis

There are several tactics that you can use to remain humble. Among them: remain connected to your people. Ensure that you know about your followers and, as often as you can, visit the front line to understand the work that you are asking your followers to do.[151] As you practice management by walking around (MBWA),[152] you will find problems that need solutions. Viewing the work that is done where the work is done is a key leadership technique.[153] This is part and parcel to being a servant, which we will discuss in greater detail in the second half of the book.

If you wait for people to come to you, you'll only get small problems.
You must go and find them.
The big problems are where people don't realise
they have one in the first place
—W. Edwards Deming[154]

---

[150] Scott 2017.

[151] In Lean system methodology, this is known as *going to gemba*, where gemba is a Japanese term meaning *the real place*. A manager goes to the real place, observes, shows respect, and seeks to understand before seeking to improve or meddle.

[152] MBWA is often credited to Hewlett Packard (HP) founders William Hewlett and David Packard, though it is a popular organizational practice and mirrors troop inspection procedures that have been in use for hundreds of years in military organizations.

[153] Peters and Waterman 1982.

[154] William Edwards Deming (1900–1993), American engineer, statistician, professor, author, and expert in the field of quality management.

There are several buzzwords that have become popular over the last few decades in leadership research. People who are highly successful, people like Richard Branson and Lee Iacocca, are undeniably big personalities. Entrepreneurs like Elon Musk have more than their fair share of charisma and perseverance in the face of long odds. It would be a logical mistake, however, to assume that charisma and perseverance are the defining characteristics of successful business people or leaders.

Oliver Burkeman in his excellent book, *The Antidote*,[155] notes that there are probably more unsuccessful people with those characteristics than successful people. People who are exceptional risk takers fail more often than they succeed. How many people visit a casino, gamble a large amount of money on a long shot, and win substantial sums of money? The answer is, of course, far fewer than those who lose at least their initial stake. Otherwise, casinos would go out of business.

Charisma is not, in and of itself, a bad thing. Transformational leaders rely on charisma and enthusiasm to motivate their followers and obtain a groundswell of support,[156] though possessing charisma alone does not make a transformational leader.[157] Charisma is not the dark side of humility; narcissism and egotism are. Many charismatic leaders are also humble. They grew up out of humble beginnings, or they understand the importance of others over self. It is often easier to follow a leader who has an excess of charisma because they are inspiring. One of the things to look out for, though, is that charismatic leaders may use this power of influence to gain a following based on their own cult of personality. Followers may be more focused on their desire to please and to follow their charismatic leader than doing what is best for the organization or its mission.

I do not mean to imply that all CEOs will be successful because they are charismatic. In fact, many leaders who are charismatic fail miserably. In his book *Good to Great: Why Some Companies Make the Leap and Others Don't*,[158] Jim Collins describes several of the CEOs of his *Good to Great* companies as humble. They are fifth-level leaders, leaders that have a number of attributes that are well defined by Collins.[159]

---

[155] Burkeman 2012.
[156] Stone, Russell, and Patterson 2004.
[157] Parry and Proctor-Thompson 2002; Bass 1985.
[158] Collins 2001a.
[159] See figure 7.

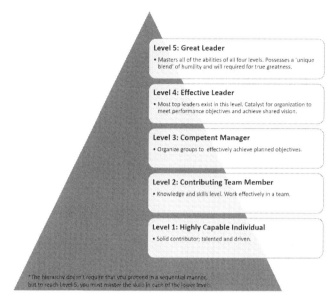

Figure 7. Collins' Level 5 hierarchy[160]

Level 5 leaders combine *deep personal humility with intense professional will* and are not typically in-your-face, large-and-in-charge celebrities but are *mild-mannered, steely leaders.*[161] Collins stops short of providing a detailed list of steps that lead to Level 5 leadership; rather, he asserts that a leader with the *seed* of Level 5 leadership should endeavor to implement the other conditions he identifies in his Good-to-Great companies.

> Don't bother trying to be better than your contemporaries or predecessors.
> Try to be better than yourself.
> —William Faulkner

There is a close relationship between humility and authenticity. These two attributes were rarely mentioned one without the other in the recent past.[162] Thomas Merton wrote extensively on finding and reconciling with one's true self. His theological work identified the need for humility in the face of dialogue with *the other*[163] and the ability to be truly focused on the *other*

---

[160] Adapted from Collins 2001b, p. 5.
[161] Collins 2001b.
[162] Vergote 1988.
[163] Merton 1972.

as a mark of humility in a leader.[164] Humility implies a self-knowledge and consequent self-acceptance that allows a leader to put another's concerns ahead of their own.[165] Humility urges us to understand and accept our strengths and limitations and, in so doing, use our strengths in service of others. A person who achieves the routine practice of humility has surpassed the *esteem* portion of Maslow's hierarchy and is well on their way to self-actualization.

A brief portion of this text should be dedicated to the idea of the transfer of power, of succession planning. Through the lens of Living Your Leadership, it is evident that with the transfer of power, humility should still play a major role.

> Do you wish to rise?
> Begin by descending.
> You plan a tower that will pierce the clouds?
> Lay first the foundation of humility.
> —Saint Augustine of Hippo

Take the history that Herodotus relates to us concerning Cyrus the Great, king of Persia, and Croesus the Lydian king[166] in about 547 BCE. Upon conquering the city of Sardis, Cyrus II sat with his prisoner, who relayed to him the folly of what he had observed occurring in his former capital, Sardis. The violent power transfer had taken place. Sardis had been taken, and Cyrus was allowing his Persian forces to sack the city and take away its treasures.

After some time in thought, Croesus questioned Cyrus about what Cyrus was seeing when he looked at the occupied city. Cyrus answered him that he saw his victorious army taking the prisoner king's wealth. Croesus looked at him and said that was not what he saw. He saw Cyrus's Persian soldiers taking Cyrus' newfound wealth from his conquered city.

This historical tale, related to us by one of the preeminent historians of the time, should be a cautionary tale for any leader that takes over a team. As they assume the reins of leadership, the leader should not try to immediately destroy the existing culture or plunder the works of the organization that they are going to lead. Rather, they should look at the accomplishments and the follies of their new organization and give due credit for the current state to the old leader. In humility, the new leader should assume the reins of leadership with their new vision of the organization firmly in mind. Oftentimes, that

---

[164] Spencer 2007.
[165] Sandage and Wiens 2001.
[166] Herodotus 2007.

means attempting a change in culture. The culture change might even mean firing and hiring new faces.

The gentility with which a leader accomplishes the change will be immediately remarked upon and long remembered.

Use your sense of humor. It is easy to take ourselves too seriously as leaders. We are in charge of people and assets and that can easily imbue a false sense of importance to our work lives. Leaders often take themselves too seriously.[167] Exercising your funny bone is freeing in that respect.

Do not take life too seriously. You willl never get out alive. – Elbert Hubbard

Figure 8. The humorless boss

Many leaders seem to think that a sense of humor is out of place in business. They would be absolutely right if they were referring only to humor that is self-deprecating, inappropriate, or demeaning. Assuming that you can draw the line between what is appropriate for the situation and what is not, humor has many tangible benefits.

1. It puts people at ease. This can be especially useful in our busy workplace. As we refuse to take ourselves too seriously, we bring a sense of levity and humility to the office.

---

[167] Vanderkam 2012.

2. Your team will benefit from the use of humor. Not only does humor help make the delivery of difficult news more palatable, but it helps get teams over the storming hump by building team cohesion.

3. Leaders who can laugh at themselves are more likeable. You do not have to be a comedian to exercise humor. Practicing an appropriate amount of humor ensures that you are not a fool but that you are someone who people want to be around.

4. Humor can be both motivating and serve to emphasize a point. Smile and laugh; your followers will smile, too.[168] People are more likely to remember a point made with a joke or a quip.

5. Humor can provide perspective. Making light of a tough situation can put struggle in perspective and allow the release of negative emotion.

6. In addition to perspective, humor can spark creativity. Creativity is a powerful cognitive force that pays huge benefits in work and life.[169]

Using humor can be a daunting prospect, especially to those introverts among us. It involves risk,[170] but the rewards far outweigh them.

A sense of humor is part of the art of leadership,
of getting along with people, of getting things done.
—Dwight D. Eisenhower

---

[168] Carnegie 1998.
[169] Csikszentmihalyi 1990.
[170] Taylor 2013.

CHAPTER RECAP

Humility is a foundational leadership practice.

- Humility is not self-effacement. It relies on an accurate understanding of self, on other-centeredness, and on social awareness.
- Humble leaders avoid self-deception and are lifelong learners.
- Listen to others with the intent to understand, not respond.
- Get out to the front line where the work happens.
- Don't be afraid of your sense of humor. You will experience greater connection and efficacy if you show your humanity using humor.

APPLICATION OF SELF-LEADERSHIP

Outstanding leaders go out of their way to boost
the self-esteem of their personnel.
If people believe in themselves, it's amazing what they can accomplish.
—Sam Walton

My first assignment was to the idyllic Central Coast of California for space and missile training. As I progressed through my technical training in space and ICBM operations, I began to think about what I needed to do to mold myself into the kind of leader I wanted to be. I started reading various books on leadership and on personal growth. I began my master's degree, and I strove to emulate the behaviors I saw in the leaders I admired around me.

Minot Air Force Base, North Dakota, was where I would call home for four long years. I was an ICBM operator and worked my way from the deputy position up to flight commander. I had operational control of approximately sixty individuals and an extraordinary amount of strategic nuclear assets. The leadership atmosphere at Minot was very much like a pressure cooker. There were constant tests and evaluations and with nearly three hundred junior officers vying for the same types of positions. Cronyism and politics undeniably played a large part in promotion. There was a major struggle to recognize merit, but all too often, there was so little quantitative difference between one junior officer and another that other factors tended to play a large role in advancement.

I had the opportunity to view leadership through the lens of high-stakes operational military leadership in Minot, North Dakota. A lot of the commanders had to deal with unenviable situations under intense scrutiny. Watching their reactions to difficult situations was more than instructive; it constituted a major paradigm shift in how I thought of leadership. In many cases, as you can imagine, draconian decisions were made in the pressure cooker environment. Mistakes were often punished way out of proportion to their actual impact. Leaders who, in less stressful situations, would have balked from meting out such severe punishment would be responsible for most heinous degradations of those below them. The thrust of many of the lessons I learned from my time in North Dakota was what *not* to do as a leader.

Of course, there were outstanding examples of humble, authentic leadership. The best leaders rise to the occasion in those kinds of environments. Unfortunately, those examples were not emulated by everyone. I had the opportunity to work with, and for, many of those incredible leaders. The level of self-sacrifice and dedication by several commanders was more than inspirational; it was life-changing.

As a self-leader, you learn to understand the rules of the social game being played and are able to determine whether or not you play those games. This simultaneous perception and choice allows followers to see that the leader is demonstrably *authentic*. Exercising that choice, making informed decisions, is a hallmark of an effective self-leader.[171]

The most prevalent form of feedback is social feedback. Part of our evolutionary makeup is the imperative to socially *fit in*. A leader is no different. Self-leadership imbues the process of self-monitoring with awareness, which allows us to notice cues from our social environment.[172] The reciprocal actions and consequences inform our future behavior in that setting. Unambiguous, plentiful, and consistent[173] feedback contributes to forming solid self-perception.

An employee receives constant feedback from coworkers and supervisors concerning task-specific performance. Social cues embedded in those communications let the employee know if the behavior conforms to acceptable group norms. That feedback reinforces the employee's role-specific social identity.

Feedback from this secondary reference group[174] is internalized and contributes substantially to the employee's perception of self. The acceptance of the feedback impacts the distance between the perceived and ideal self,

---

[171] Bryant and Kazan 2013, p. 41.
[172] Gardner and Cole 1988.
[173] Leonard, Beauvais, and Scholl 1995, p. 323.
[174] Primary reference groups are typically family units.

which informs self-esteem in an iterative, social process.[175, 176] In the same way that your self-concept is impacted by the praise, acceptance, or criticism of others, your followers will be affected. With that understanding in mind, you should seek to employ the lessons learned about self-leadership to leading your followers.

In his social cognitive theory, Albert Bandura examines self-regulatory processes in a social milieu. He noted that people have greater motivation to change when the results of their social learning is positively appreciated by their social group.[177] One of the most common ways that positive appreciation of change is accomplished is through recognition.

Recognition can be a double-edged sword; it can make people feel good and enhance their intrinsic motivation, but the extrinsic nature of recognition can have negative psychological ramifications. From a behaviorist perspective, if recognition is administered in a manner that is consistent with a particular desired behavior, then it becomes a contingent reward; transactional in nature.[178] A contingent reward serves to stimulate an individual's extrinsic motivation while causing a slide in the locus of control from an internal one to an external one. This decrease in intrinsic motivation is an undesirable long-term outcome.

Prior to rewarding behavioral change, focus on the effect that praise will have on an individual and on the group. Attempt to catch a follower in the act that you would like to recognize and reward. If an award is given in a spontaneous manner in front of subordinates and superiors, it is more likely to positively motivate.[179, 180]

A reward should be temporally close to the event itself to increase the perception of relevance of the reward to the action for the individual. Even a small good behavior, when recognized, can have a huge impact on their future performance.[181] There can be a transactional element to verbal praise,[182] and so we should carefully regulate our offering of praise to make sure it does not become the carrot in the extrinsic stick-and-carrot approach to behavior management.

---

[175] Leonard, Beauvais, and Scholl 1995.

[176] Bandura 1986.

[177] Bryant and Kazan 2013, p. 16.

[178] Bass 1985.

[179] Cameron, Pierce, Banko, and Gear 2005.

[180] Deci, Connell, and Ryan 1989.

[181] Poore 2012.

[182] Yukl 1999.

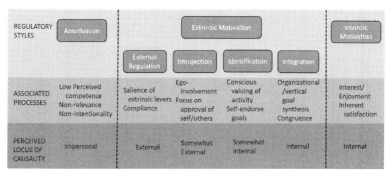

REGULATORY STYLES	Amotivation	Extrinsic Motivation				Intrinsic Motivation
		External Regulation	Introjection	Identification	Integration	
ASSOCIATED PROCESSES	Low Perceived competence Non-relevance Non-intentionality	Salience of extrinsic levers Compliance	Ego-involvement Focus on approval of self/others	Conscious valuing of activity Self-endorse goals	Organizational /vertical goal synthesis Congruence	Interest/ Enjoyment Inherent satisfaction
PERCEIVED LOCUS OF CAUSALITY	Impersonal	External	Somewhat External	Somewhat Internal	Internal	Internal

Figure 9. A taxonomy of human motivation[183]

Should an individual receive praise often compared to their peers, then it may be a good idea to encourage them in a different manner. You may choose to encourage the awardee to coach fellow employees in the behaviors that they are routinely praised for, for instance. Encouragement should be more often applied to those who would benefit from it, the mid to low achievers, though genuine appreciation should be given freely and often.[184]

Valuing individuals should become ingrained to the point where it is an entirely ubiquitous part of organizational culture, much in the same way as expressed by the Disney paradigm: *gratitude improves attitude*. Disney renamed their employees *cast members* and affords them the respect and responsibility to make a difference.[185]

This paradigm shift involves seeing employees with compassion. For example, do not think, *My manning is strained because Larry is taking too much time off. Rather, Larry has been having a rough time with his custody agreement and needs some time for his family. Maybe we should write him a sympathy card and offer him counseling resources.* Recognition works the same way. "Sandy just finished her MA in education. We should celebrate her life achievement!" Though it is not of any financial value to the organization, Sandy just accomplished something laudable and deserves recognition from her leaders. Small, individualized recognition can make a large impact on an employee's outlook and effort.

When a genuine accomplishment is earned by a high achiever, it is sometimes not credited so that others will not feel unappreciated in comparison. This is a mistake. Failing to recognize that person has a negative

---

[183] *Adapted from Ryan and Deci 2000.
[184] Cashman 2008.
[185] Poore 2012.

effect on overall morale and motivation. By refusing to acknowledge genuinely impressive accomplishments as they happen, the overall expectations for the group are lowered. Less impressive performance starts to be seen in the same light as truly exceptional performance. This removes the motivational incentive to struggle for exceptional achievement when the simply adequate will earn the same recognition. It makes no logical sense to reward mediocre performance, just as it makes no sense to punish your highly motivated performers.

There is a positive effect when appropriate and timely recognition is applied to low achievers. Transference of confidence is known as the Pygmalion or Rosenthal effect.[186] A teacher or other adult, someone who believes in a person's innate potential, causes that person to flourish based on that positive expectation. This is a transfer of confidence. A leader can have the same effect on their followers. A leader who truly believes and expresses confidence in the potential and abilities of their followers will inspire confidence in those followers.

How leaders handle adversity, their ability to find meaning in negative events and yet push forward, is an indication of perseverance. Take a traumatic situation and look at it as a learning experience. Focus on the positive effect, if there are any. Those leaders who can do that and come away stronger are better leaders for it.[187]

> Between stimulus and response, there is space.
> In that space is our power to choose our response.
> In our response lies our growth and our freedom.
> —Viktor E. Frankl

I would be remiss if I didn't mention the 90/10 rule while discussing choice of attitude, positivity, and motivation. As the quote from Viktor Frankl states, there is a space where you can react to a situation, and that choice is freedom. His internment in a concentration camp is certainly a much starker reality than any situation we will ever find ourselves in.[188] Frankl's ideas about the search for meaning gave rise to his theory of logotherapy. Logotherapy revolves around the pursuit of meaning for a person's life.

Steven Covey popularized the 90/10 rule. He is one of the most popular

---

[186] Bryant and Kazan 2013, p. 68.

[187] Bennis and Thomas 2002b.

[188] Viktor Frankl (1905–1997) was an Austrian neurologist and psychiatrist and the inventor of logotherapy. Between 1942 and 1945, he labored in four Nazi concentration camps, including Auschwitz. His parents, brother, and pregnant wife perished in the Holocaust.

thinkers in the management and leadership development sphere, having authored several *New York Times* best sellers on those subjects. The 90/10 rule is a bit less complex and more widely applicable than many of the other practical applications of psychological theories for management and leadership. In life and in leadership, 10 percent of what happens to you is out of your control, and 90 percent of a situation is your reaction to it.

This is most applicable for leaders. Leaders are constantly on display. Their reactions to anything from policy change, to criticism, to organizational change determine what followers' reactions will be. One of your employees accidentally splashed hot coffee on your shirt as you turned a corner. Would you curse? Would you glare? Would you take that brief moment described by Victor Frankl and choose to react in a way that will speak to your leadership practice? This is a deliberately easy example.

Consider this scenario: Your executive has decided not to fund your pet project. You find out about her decision just prior to your morning meeting. All of your employees and your management team attend this meeting and look to you for leadership. Will you allow that negative situation, that rejection, to color your attitude?

Your first thought before you enter the room full of your followers must be, *I am their leader. They look to me for motivation, for guidance.* Your attitude at this meeting could very well shape the rest of their interactions for that day and beyond. Reflect on the overall objective of your work unit. Consider that there are always other ways to address rejected ideas, and perhaps solicit ideas from your staff to counter the rejection. This, in turn, involves and empowers your employees. Consequently, involving your followers in the process increases their intrinsic motivation to perform by increasing their perceived autonomy because they want to help someone who looked to them for assistance.

The 90/10 rule is more than just a reminder to be on your best behavior. It is a lesson that you should keep in mind at all times. It is something to ingrain in your daily practice to the point where it becomes second nature. Remember that your response determines the outcome of events, rather than the event determining your response. You are in control of your attitude by choice.

You have the freedom and, as the leader, the obligation to respond appropriately.

CHAPTER RECAP

Self-leaders are humble and authentic. They understand social cues and have an unshakeable understanding and appreciation of self.

- Encourage and practice feedback.
- Employ feedback and reward in such a way that it serves to increase intrinsic motivation in your followers.
- Though your leadership endeavors might be difficult, endeavor to persevere.
- Learn to choose your reaction to situations.

Leadership is all about people.
It is not about organizations.
It is not about plans.
It is not about strategies.
It is all about people—motivating people to get the job done.
You have to be people-centered.
—Colin Powell

LEADING OTHERS

MANAGEMENT VERSUS LEADERSHIP

Management is the most noble of professions if it's practiced well. No other occupation offers as many ways to help others learn and grow, take responsibility and be recognized for achievement, and contribute to the success of a team.[189]
—Clayton M. Christensen[190]

Labor negotiations had started. The atmosphere in every biomed shop in Northern California had been tense for months. Some major, unpopular changes had reduced overtime and impacted fringe benefits like use of company vehicles. The talk of strike abounded, and sympathy strikes had already garnered more support than usual from the usually reticent crowd of engineers.

I was excited, though. I had been involved in many of the changes that had occurred, planning and executing some of them as the project management lead. My boss, we'll call him Steve, had authorized me to be present during the opening stages of negotiations as a subject matter expert, and I couldn't have been more pleased to learn about the inner workings of the negotiation process.

After I parked, checked my appearance in the reflection of my car (I was wearing one of the few suits I owned at the time and was nervous about how it looked on me), and grabbed my case full of related files, I walked toward the entrance of the union headquarters. I was met halfway by Steve and his

---

[189] http://hbr.org/2010/07/how-will-you-measure-your-life/ar/2.
[190] Clayton Magleby Christensen, professor of business administration at the Harvard Business School and acknowledged expert on innovation and growth.

boss (the executive). Without looking at me, the executive turned to Steve and inaudibly spoke to him for a minute before turning away and walking into the building. To his credit, Steve looked chagrined when he told me that I wasn't welcome at negotiations. Despite having been cleared to attend by all parties, the executive had a new plan that did not involve me being present at negotiations.

I was stunned. Not because I wasn't allowed to attend anymore, though that was disappointing, but by the fact that the executive, who I had dinner with in the past and who had sent me to specialized training, didn't deign to speak to me himself. It was the casual dismissiveness that crushed any vestiges of loyalty I held for him in that moment. Steve was not off the hook at that point, either. He didn't speak a word in my defense, just relayed the message without apology, turned his back, and walked into the building. I was left, holding my injured feelings and my case bulging with union documents, in the parking lot.

Thus far, this book has been concerned with the development of self. A leader is not fit to lead if they cannot first lead themselves. The development of self is not a step on the ladder to successfully Living Your Leadership. It is the foundation of your leadership practice. Without it, your leadership would be based on only external understanding.

Ultimately, leadership is about others. There is a necessary reciprocal relationship between the leader and the follower.[191] The maintenance of that relationship defines leadership practice.

> In *Managers and Leaders: Are They Different?*, I argued that a crucial difference between managers and leaders lies in the conceptions they hold, deep in their psyches, of chaos and order. Leaders tolerate chaos and lack of structure and are prepared to keep answers in suspense, avoiding premature closure on important issues. Managers seek order and control and are almost compulsively addicted to disposing of problems even before they understand their potential significance. In my experience, seldom do the uncertainties of potential chaos cause problems. Instead, it is the instinctive moved to impose order on potential chaos that makes trouble for organizations. (Abraham Zaleznik)

---

[191] Kouzes and Posner 1989.

Moving on to the study of leadership practices focusing primarily on others, there are several extant, popular theories. In this text, the focus will be on transformational leadership and servant leadership. Both of these theories have deep grounding in scholarly research and literature and are put into practice by some of the world's most successful business and spiritual leaders.

I had the unique opportunity to serve in Mosul, Iraq, as an electronic warfare officer liaising with the army. Going from a high-stakes, pressure cooker environment in Minot, North Dakota, to a leadership environment where lives are consistently on the line was an eye-opening change for me. My responsibility was to ensure the proper operation of signal-jamming devices that defeated improvised explosive devices the enemy would set for radio detonation.

Each time a convoy would drive off the FOB (forward operating base), a piece of my soul would go with them. Knowing that the education I provided those soldiers operating and maintaining their jamming devices would inevitably either save or, if they chose to disregard it, end their lives brought the idea of servant leadership sharply into perspective for me. I would often seek the opportunity to roll out with convoys so I could see the equipment while it was operating and emphasize the importance of its use.

Management is efficiency in climbing the ladder of success;
leadership determines whether the ladder is leaning against the right wall.
—Stephen Covey

There is a foundational understanding of management and leadership that begs wider acceptance and understanding. Management and leadership are two different concepts. A simple litmus test for management versus leadership practice is whether a robot could do the job with the appropriate programming. If the answer is yes, I have bad news for you. Managers control processes, while leaders empower and influence people. It is a near-universal experience in the working world to have had a boss who acts only as a manager and rarely as a leader.

Managers were scarce in the Iraqi area of operations. While engaged in combat operations and planning, I met leaders at all ranks, from different countries, and from different military services. These men and women led from the front. They did not shy away from their duty. I watched some of them bravely perish and others compassionately inspire their troops in the wake of disaster.

> Leaders have the ability to inspire others to achieve
> what managers say is not feasible.
> —Colin Powell

One of the main tasks of leadership is developing and communicating vision. Leaders define the future organizational vision and goals. Management is the transportation system meant to mechanically move the organization from current state to future state. Leadership defines the change, shows the way, and sets the organizational destination. Management is task oriented and works to achieve the vision leaders have clearly defined. There is always a need to manage processes, but leadership is indispensable to the successful organization.

There are practices relating solely to the two theories mentioned above outlined in the following chapters. In addition, curated practices that most closely align with the internal work accomplished in the first half of the book will be mentioned, whether or not they particularly apply to either transformational or servant leadership. Place the focus of leadership practice on others only after an effort has been made to conform to the theory-to-practice outlined in the *self*-portion of the text.

> Before you are a leader, success is all about growing yourself.
> When you become a leader, success is all about growing others.
> —Jack Welch

Transformational leadership is one of the two theories that Living Your Leadership hinges on when practicing other-centeredness. In 1978, Sir MacGregor Burns identified that leaders were either transactional or transformational.[192] The understanding of that concept has evolved over time to recognize that leaders operate on a continuum from transactional to transformational leadership styles. Transformational leadership characteristics include many that are also identified as positive characteristics of servant leadership. In those cases of behavioral overlap, the terms *transformational* and *servant* may be used interchangeably.

Measures of leadership effectiveness are often outcome measures. Outcome measures are based on profit and loss or other quantifiable measures of organizational success. If you've gotten this far in this book, then you probably understand that organizational success isn't the penultimate measure

---

[192] Burns 1978.

of success as a leader. A leader must also be able to empathize, to treat followers with respect, and to lead with humility.

Leaders with high emotional intelligence (EQ) may not be the most successful leaders,[193] but that may not have anything to do with their high EQ. Rather, it may result from other qualities and habits of that individual. Does a leader need to be emotionally intelligent? Traits that point to high emotional intelligence like self-awareness and empathy are essential to Living Your Leadership. Leaders with high EQ are passionate and logical, seamlessly combining emotions with intelligence.[194] This is a major point of intersection between the practice of transformational leadership and Living Your Leadership.

A true meritocracy promotes individuals who excel—those who prove themselves through superior performance. Without a meritocracy, an unhealthy skepticism in the abilities of coworkers who may have been promoted for reasons other than performance may develop. Promotion based on seniority may appeal to the lazy and entitled, but it is not the hallmark of an effective organization.

In some organizations, promotion is based on seniority or politicking. Milestones like promotion or being chosen for specialized training would normally serve to reinforce positive self-efficacy beliefs. When they are handed out too often or without an obvious connection to effort on the part of the recipient, the motivational benefits are undermined for the recipient and for those who bear witness.

Traditional models of leadership are typically autocratic and hierarchical. These are clearly outdated and detrimental to quick, clear, and effective communication.[195] The flattening of the organizational structure and the decentralization of power is critical to empowering followers in an organization. Imbuing followers with the authority, resources, and responsibility,[196] while maintaining ultimate accountability in the hands of the leader, will empower employees to achieve organizational outcomes. Autocratic leadership is an anathema to the Living Your Leadership paradigm, wherein followers are encouraged to participate in decision-making processes.

---

[193] Lindebaum and Cartwright 2011.
[194] Spencer 2007.
[195] Cockerell 2008.
[196] Winston 2003.

	URGENT	NOT URGENT
IMPORTANT	**DO** Get this done ASAP	**DECIDE** Put this on your schedule
NOT IMPORTANT	**DELEGATE** Can someone do it for you?	**DELETE** If you have time...

Figure 10. The Eisenhower box

The Eisenhower box is a concrete representation of the way that a leader acts in response to tasks. Every one of us has a lot of things to do; that is an immutable rule of our times. We are no longer peasant farmers ruled by a feudal lord; we are leaders in the information technology age. Many leaders receive hundreds of emails per day, are in charge of dozens of people, and have multiple projects in our primary occupations. Add those responsibilities to the effort and care owed to family, social, and spiritual life.

Leaders are jugglers with too many flaming machetes up in the air. The Eisenhower box is one way to organize decision-making processes for maximum efficiency. Dwight Eisenhower said, "What is important is seldom urgent, and what is urgent is seldom important." This tool allows a leader to address those things that require action in a structured way.

Effective leadership is putting first things first.
Effective management is discipline, carrying it out.
—Stephen Covey

Have you ever sat back and wondered what is actually important in your life? Of those things, how much time do you spend on each compared with those things that you immediately rejected as unimportant? Would you rank personal growth among those things that are unimportant? That is unlikely.

If we can agree that growth is important, how much time and energy are you putting toward it each day? Each week? Do you have an overall plan or strategy that you were pursuing? These types of questions have a direct bearing on whether you are pursuing your leadership journey with *intention*.

A common aphorism for leadership is that leaders take all of the blame and none of the credit. Try to avoid any scenario where the words *all* or *none* are used in most circumstances. Using absolutes precludes the possibility of alternative solutions. In this case, it is important to recognize that leaders must be in the habit of accepting blame and distributing credit. By accepting blame, a leader shields employees from repercussions from above and makes them feel safe and trusted.

An employee who feels trusted also feels able to contribute through moderate risk taking and innovation. These behaviors can raise the level of team performance to new heights while at the same time strengthening the bonds of trust between the leader and the follower. You are already the leader—why do you need credit, other than to feed your ego? Allowing others to have credit for successful initiatives means that they are more likely to take the initiative in future situations.

Additionally, engendering trust, taking blame, and distributing credit promotes a sense of self-worth and leads to the creation of other leaders, which is one of the distinguishing factors of leadership itself.[197] Advancing your people, expanding their leadership horizons, and building them into leaders themselves is not only a success for them but is also a success for you as a leader. Robert Greenleaf established that the best test for servant leadership success, and the most difficult to administer, is asking whether those served grow as persons.

Louis Efron asserts that ensuring a lasting and successful organization means that there must be foundational leadership at the core of the organization. He goes on to describe the three main parts of *foundational leadership* as establishing trust, demonstrating care, and practicing servant leadership.[198] His emphasis on transparency and integrity are crucial to the practice of Living Your Leadership. Of special note, transparency and integrity both relate to authenticity in the paradigm.

Don't be afraid to show your vulnerability. Be transparent with your team, even when the truth may be unpopular or inconvenient.
—Bill George

---

[197] "The function of leadership is to produce more leaders, not more followers" (Ralph Nader).
[198] Efron 2015.

You have to be honest and authentic and not hide. I think the leader today has to demonstrate both transparency and vulnerability, and with that comes truthfulness and humility.

—Howard Schultz[199]

Managers and leaders take different approaches to their work. Managers have problems that need to be solved, just like leaders. Managers use an impersonal approach when responding to problems, seeking first to manage by exception (MBE). That is, correcting the mistake in the process as it occurs, rather than taking a holistic view of the situation. Leaders are active instead of reactive. A leader sits with chaos calmly instead of responding immediately. A leader seeks to understand before applying a solution. Leadership demands adaptation of personal approach and maintaining an active posture toward goals and problems.[200]

While leaders plan ahead, managers are more reactive to their surroundings. Strategically minded leaders look beyond today and set processes in place to prevent negative outcomes from occurring. Today's information economy requires leaders, rather than managers. Leaders intentionally and actively mentor their employees, they strategically plan, and they genuinely care about the people side of the organization. Leaders are not afraid to interact meaningfully with their followers. A leader is willing to have the difficult conversation when necessary. They are able to inspire their team, to teach, and to develop their followers.

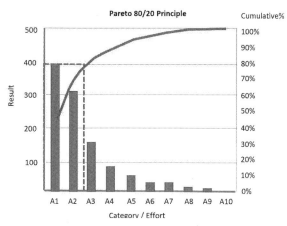

Figure 11. Pareto graph

---

[199] CEO of Starbucks.
[200] Zaleznik 1992.

If you have had the opportunity to attend any Six Sigma or other process improvement training, then you are probably aware of the Pareto principle. The Pareto principle is an observation, not a scientific law. The idea behind the Pareto principle is that results are not always evenly distributed. Originally, the Pareto principle was an observation that 80 percent of the land in Italy was concentrated in 20 percent of the people.[201] Observing the chart above, you'll notice that roughly 80 percent of the results are due to only about 20 percent of the effort expended, categories A1 and A2. This means that 80 percent of your success during the day is only related to about 20 percent of your effort.

This principle can apply to almost anything during your day as a leader. It has been said that 20 percent of the people that you lead will take 80 percent of your time. Perhaps you have also observed that 20 percent of your tasks take 80 percent of your time. After the first 20 percent of effort is expended, producing 80 percent of the results, any additional effort makes less of a difference than the first 20 percent did. In economics, this is referred to as the law of diminishing returns.

It should be noted that the last 20 percent is not unnecessary. Rather, you should take time when analyzing the tasks that you have to perform to determine which are the most important and which can wait. This is much like the Eisenhower box; it is a valuable tool to save time for more important tasks.

---

[201] It was named after Italian economist Vilfredo Pareto in or around 1906.

CHAPTER RECAP

Leadership is ultimately about others. Transformational and servant leadership theory guide the second half of this text.

- Manage processes, not people. Leaders have vision; mangers have metrics.
- Traditional leadership often involved hierarchies and direct orders. Transformational and servant leaders work through influence, with an emphasis on the needs of others and the character of the leader.
- A leader engenders trust, takes blame, and distributes credit. They delegate tasks and develop their followers.

RESPECT AND HUMAN DIGNITY

The essential qualities and values that enable one person
to influence others & the capacity to reach and touch one
another as caring, compassionate human beings.
—David Lawrence, MD, Former Chairman and
CEO, Kaiser Foundation Health Plan, Inc.

A major change initiative was afoot in the missile operations field. The question raised was whether it would be safer and more efficient to conduct alerts that lasted three days rather than one day. This wasn't the first time this particular question had been raised, but, organizational memory being what it is, the question was asked again. There were concerns before, and there were concerns with this implementation.

Logistically, a three-day alert would mean that a squadron would send three operators out to each of their ten missile sites for seventy-two hours instead of two operators per site for twenty-four hours. One of the three squadrons in the wing had been volunteered to participate in the pilot effort by its commander. This decision was wildly unpopular with the entire crew force.

There were a lot of unanswered questions about the transition and about the execution of the new schedule. One of the major causes of discomfort and fear revolved around concern about the impact on families. This new alert structure dictated a minimum of eighty hours away from home at a time, most often with only a day and a half off before going right back out on alert.

A commander's call was held prior to implementation of the

seventy-two-hour alert structure. A commander's call is akin to an all-hands staff meeting. The missile field does not sleep. Each day, at least ten missileers from each squadron, so ten people at the meeting and ten people in the missile field, received the news just before or during their alert activity. At this meeting, complaints regarding the impact to families were raised to the commander. Rather than hearing, empathizing, and validating the concerns of his multitude of followers, he responded with "If the air force had wanted you to have a family, it would have issued you one." Dead silence followed. Whether or not he meant what he said, the words couldn't be unsaid, and more importantly, they couldn't be unheard. He had communicated his lack of respect for the dignity of his followers all too clearly, and the results were catastrophic.

Emotions are an important part of people. Ignoring or invalidating the feelings of others is a violation of their dignity and constitutes a disrespectful behavior on the part of a leader. Especially in the military, however, feelings do not trump operational requirements. That is not the point here at all. It is imperative that a leader take the time to acknowledge, empathize, and thereby validate the emotions of followers. Had that commander taken the time to listen to the concerns of his followers, he would have been able to validate their concerns.

> One of the most sincere forms of respect is actually
> listening to what another has to say.
> —Bryant McGill[202]

Empathy and validation may not dictate any change in the actions a leader takes, but they should play a role in the decision-making process. Caring behaviors are inherently ethical,[203] and they enhance the growth of employees, in addition to improving the quality of an organization's culture.[204]

> There is a deep—and usually frustrated—desire in the heart of
> everyone to act with benevolence rather than selfishness, and
> one fine instance of generosity can inspire dozens more.
> Thus I established a stately court where all my friends showed respect to
> each other and cultivated courtesy until it bloomed into perfect harmony.
> —Cyrus the Great

---

[202] UN-appointed Global Champion and Nobel Peace Prize nominee.

[203] Brown and Treviño 2006.

[204] Spears 2010, p. 26.

If you took a moment right now to think back to the best leader you've ever had, would you reminisce about how valued you felt if they yelled at you first thing in the morning? Would you look fondly back on the times that you were berated for not having done precisely what they expect you to do, but never told you precisely how to do? I think it is far more likely that your ideal leader would have encouraged you, communicated expectations clearly, and supported your personhood in addition to supporting your work.

Expectations run both ways. Keeping that in mind, here are some of the important expectations of leaders from experienced followers:[205]

1. Get out of your comfort zone and actually visit people who are doing the job. A visible leader inspires.

2. Leaders make mistakes; acknowledge and grow from them. Without that acknowledgment of error, it is unlikely that anyone will believe that you are authentic.

3. Leaders communicate with, not to, followers. Communication both up and down the chain of command will result in inclusion and transparency. Exercise and encourage candor, ensuring that you create an atmosphere of trust and nonretribution; forthrightness may be uncomfortable, but it is necessary to encourage feedback that fuels change.[206]

4. Empower individuals by including them and distributing authority appropriately. As you invest authority in your followers, be certain that you are not micromanaging. Micromanaging implies a lack of faith in your subordinates and those you have entrusted with your authority.

5. Live your values and espouse the organization's ethical standards.

The value of a person (not only to the organization but in and of themselves) should not be based solely on their professional or personal achievements. Of the many follower-oriented leadership theories, both servant and self-sacrificial leadership share other-centeredness as a main subset of the attitudinal dimension, with valuing people encompassed by that trait.[207]

Intrinsic motivation is built on autonomy. Self-concept is based on competency beliefs, ego, and the feedback environment. Employees will exercise

---

[205] Goldfein 1999.
[206] Lorenz 2012.
[207] Matteson and Irving 2006.

autonomy if encouraged by the organizational culture and the leadership style of the management staff.[208]

It is not enough to simply appreciate the work that an employee does. A person is not a product. Their efforts are valuable, and they are more than a cog in a wheel. While critical to the organization's success, anyone is replaceable. On a purely human level, they are not replaceable. People instinctively and inherently desire respect for their effort and for their individuality.[209]

People want to be cared for.[210] If they have loved ones, those loved ones deserve a leader's consideration as well. Employees who are cared for will work harder and produce better results.[211] Consequent to your care and compassion, employees will overlook your faults.[212]

Leaders are accountable to those they lead. Leaders are responsible for the consequences of the decisions they make. More importantly, leaders are accountable for followers' decisions.[213] This is something that no leader should ever take for granted or forget.

There is an unspoken but powerful contract between the leader and their followers. The implicit agreement is that the leader will care for the followers, that their mental and physical well-being will supersede the leader's own. Additionally, the leader is responsible for the promotion and growth of their followers. The idea that the leader is accountable for those they lead forms the basis of their mutual relational contract.

The leader acknowledges that the basic humanity of their followers is the same as their own. Position may separate the leader from the follower, but a title does not imply superiority.

> Whatever is my right as a man is also the right of another;
> and it becomes my duty to guarantee as well as to possess.
> —Thomas Paine, *Rights of Man*

The realization of the equality of leaders and followers should bring to mind the idea of humility. Leaders are in the position to positively influence their followers and are placed in a position of authority over them, despite their inherent equality. The takeaway here is twofold: leaders should understand

[208] Bryant and Kazan 2013, p. 34.
[209] Welch and Welch 2005, p. 53.
[210] Noddings 1998.
[211] Blanchard and Johnson 1982.
[212] Lorenz 2012.
[213] Lorenz 2012.

that (1) they have the honor of serving their followers and (2) with the privilege of leading comes the responsibility to lead well.

From everyone who has been given much, much will be demanded;
and from the one who has been entrusted with
much, much more will be asked.
—Luke 12:48 ASV

You cannot just say that you believe in the value of people. Living Your Leadership embraces the fundamental principle underlying servant leadership—that every person is part of a team and is valuable regardless of their title or position.[214] A leader must suit action to words. If a leader says they value people, their actions must confirm it beyond any doubt.

Figure 12. Authority crushes autonomy

Authority is the last resort of the inept.
—Chip R. Bell[215]

---

[214] Page and Wong 2000.
[215] Chip Bell is a customer loyalty consultant and best-selling author.

I was demoted from my position as flight commander before being sent to Iraq. Not by my boss, though. My boss' boss decided that an example needed to be made.[216] I was one of three flight commanders in a squadron that had just had a serious operational screwup. None of my subordinates were involved. Since I was the longest tenured flight commander, however, this colonel decided it would send a strict message to his followers and his bosses to terminate someone.

His rationale was that there had been a breakdown of the ever-important *compliance mind-set* and that those in charge (not his boss, or him, or his subordinate leaders, mind you) had promulgated a culture of noncompliance. Under those pretenses, I was demoted and happily accepted my opportunity to go make a difference in Iraq.

I was well respected and one of the most trusted leaders in the larger group at the time. My commander had rated me as his top junior officer. My team had been recognized time and again for performance, and the site under my command had recently been awarded as the best launch control center at the base. None of that mattered to the leader who needed to send a message.

Top-down leadership is not uncommon in the military. Structure and discipline often demand it. When a leader cannot trust discipline to their subordinate leaders, when a leader chooses punishment to manipulate political perception, that leader has dropped an anvil on their follower.

> Man's personal dignity requires besides that he enjoy freedom and be able to make up his own mind when he acts. In his association with his fellows, therefore, there is every reason why his recognition of rights, observance of duties, and many-sided collaboration with other men, should be primarily a matter of his own personal decision. Each man should act on his own initiative, conviction, and sense of responsibility, not under the constant pressure of external coercion or enticement. There is nothing human about a society that is welded together by force. Far from encouraging, as it should, the attainment of man's progress and perfection, it is merely an obstacle to his freedom. (John XXIII[217])

---

[216] Side note: if you ever think to yourself, *I'm going to punish someone so that an example of my righteous judgment can be attested to by the rest of my followers*, you should critically examine your motivation to lead.

[217] Catholic Church 1963, p. 34.

Ultimately, top-down leadership is detrimental to the servant leadership paradigm. Top-down leadership means that authority is applied directly from management onto the employees below (like monkeys in a tree). Just as this mental image suggests, the exercise of that direct control means that followers have very little opportunity to grow.

> You don't lead by hitting people over the head.
> That's assault, not leadership.
> —Dwight D. Eisenhower

Persuasion is the tool of the successful leader. While many historically successful leaders have used positional authority (especially monarchs and military commanders), leaders in collaborative environments attempt to convince rather than direct. Influence drives consensus more assuredly than a well-reasoned argument. Leaders who choose to lead by external incentives and punishments will negate creativity, passion, and dedication in their employees. Generous compensation packages are not necessarily the fastest or most effective path to career fulfillment.[218]

> A genuine leader is not a searcher for consensus, but a molder of consensus.
> —Martin Luther King Jr.

Negative feedback is necessary for poor performance. Negative feedback does not have to mean punishment. In fact, when a leader believes in the employee, negative feedback will inspire performance. The willingness of an employee to accept guidance during a negative feedback session and the likelihood of the leader to guide the employee in a positive direction depend greatly on the feedback environment in an organization.

The feedback environment is defined by an organization's leadership. It is more than the sum of feedback sessions and annual performance reports; it consists of both planned and spontaneous verbal affirmation, positional promotions, and monetary and other performance-based rewards. Subtler but no less impactful, the feedback environment is influenced by Living Your Leadership. The relationships you have developed with your followers colors the feedback environment, ensuring that it is authentic and resonant.

Leading and managing are hardly synonymous. One of the major differences you will find is the penchant for appearance over substance.

---

[218] Pink 2012.

Managers who are more concerned with the political perception of themselves than with their reputation amongst their followers are more common than anyone would like to believe.

> We should be slow to speak and patient in listening to all ...
> Our ears should be wide open to our neighbor
> until he seems to have said all that is in his mind.
> —St. Ignatius Loyola

As an admitted leadership studies aficionado, one of the first things I do when I am invited into the office of a leader is to check out their book collection. It isn't uncommon for someone at the upper-management level to have a small, curated collection to impress others, visibly represent their own leadership philosophy, and potentially read in moments of peace or passion. In some cases, the books are fairly generic, ubiquitous to an organization. Other times, the books I've seen on the shelves of military commanders and civilian senior leaders have shocked me. I knew, for example, that I probably wouldn't get along with the base commander who had Niccolo Machiavelli's *The Prince* prominently displayed on his shelf. It was not a surprise, therefore, when he applied the principles of that amoral, political being in his leadership practice.

During my combat deployment to Iraq in 2008–2009, I was required to play host to distinguished visitors (DVs) from the air force. This was my duty because I was the senior-ranking air force officer present on the FOB. This base was primarily an army base that played host to multinational forces and had responsibility for the largest area of responsibility (AOR) in Iraq at the time.

Among the visitors who came to the FOB were an air force general and his staff. All told, there were nearly ten individuals following the general, including his aide-de-camp, a major. I met them in the late morning, immediately after checking a convoy's electronic warfare equipment so that they could *roll outside the wire*.[219] Based on the job that I was performing at the time, working with electrical equipment, I had to wear flame-retardant clothing, and the only pieces I had were army-issued camouflage. I had emailed and phoned my counterparts and my liaison in-country for air force approved uniform pieces rated for flame retardancy and was told to simply wear whatever the army provided. I acquiesced happily because it helped me fit in with the thousands of army soldiers I worked around.

After the several-hour visit was concluded, the major came up to me and

---

[219] From the relative safety of the FOB into enemy-controlled, marginal, or contested territory.

chastised me, on behalf of the general, for not wearing an air force uniform during his visit. On a normal occasion, stateside, I might have taken the feedback seriously. No one wants to disappoint a high-ranking officer in their own service, after all. However, in the middle of a combat zone, when wasting my time chauffeuring around a crew of noncombatants only to have them criticize my choice of apparel was demeaning and infuriating. Appearance over substance.

> 1930. Respect for the human person entails respect for the rights that flow from his dignity as a creature. These rights are prior to society and must be recognized by it. They are the basis of the moral legitimacy of every authority: by flouting them, or refusing to recognize them in its positive legislation, a society undermines its own moral legitimacy. If it does not respect them, authority can rely only on force or violence to obtain obedience from its subjects ...

> 1931. Respect for the human person proceeds by way of respect for the principle that "everyone should look upon his neighbor (without any exception) as *another self*, above all bearing in mind his life and the means necessary for living it with dignity." (CCC[220])

---

[220] Catholic Church 1995, part 3, section 1, chapter 2, article 3, 1930–1931.

CHAPTER RECAP

Leaders give a damn about their people. They care greatly about them as individuals in addition to appreciating the work that they do on a daily basis.

- Encourage your followers and thoughtfully communicate expectations.
- Leaders are ultimately accountable.
- Leaders grow their people.
- The feedback environment should be defined by the leader. Affirmation of the value of the person does not mean that poor performance should be allowed to persist. Rather, transparent communication about performance deficits are necessary for improvement.
- Leaders prefer substance over appearance; they are authentic.

LEADING WITH EMPATHY

No one cares how much you know, until they know how much you care.
—Theodore Roosevelt

If I had to choose a leader that I came into personal contact with that embodies empathy and servanthood, it would be Colonel Marné Deranger. I had the opportunity to work for Colonel Deranger after I came back from my combat deployment in Iraq. She did not know me. She had only the word of the person that I worked for at the time and whatever information she could glean from my performance reports up to that point.

I was not the traditional acquisition for that position. There were certain criteria that were understood as necessary prerequisites to becoming an ICBM operations instructor. Among those was that I had been exposed to teaching in an operational position. My career had taken me a different route while I was stationed at Minot, North Dakota, and I had followed what is typically referred to as the leadership route, having been promoted from a line operator to assistant flight commander to flight commander before being deployed.

I did have the advantage of already having a master's degree in education and had started pursuing my PhD at that point, but because I didn't serve in the training squadron while at Minot AFB, I had surrendered myself to the idea that I would not qualify for one of my dream positions as an instructor. You can imagine my shock and gratitude when I received my acceptance letter, signed by Colonel Deranger, while I was sitting in my containerized housing unit in Mosul, Iraq.

Upon my return to the United States from Iraq, I started my tenure as an instructor. I was on cloud nine. Living on the beautiful Central Coast of California and teaching ICBM operations was a dream come true! I still vividly remembered the first time I signed for control of nuclear weapons while on crew in North Dakota, and I was excited to imbue my students with that enthusiasm and with the lessons that I had learned in the frozen north.

I knew there was something different about Colonel Deranger when I first walked into her office at Vandenberg Air Force Base, California, in April 2009. She greeted me at her door smiling, on time for our appointment. She asked me what I needed to make the transition successful and inquired about my family before she concerned herself with the value that I would add to her organization.

Every chance I got from then on, I studied her actions and her words and found that they were always congruent. She would remember the names of people's children, inquire after our opinion about how best to proceed with operational issues, and make herself available at any time should an emergency arise.

I count myself as extremely privileged to have served under someone who truly embraced a servant leadership culture. Especially in the environment of a teaching institution where we trained warfighters in the world's most destructive technologies, her brand of other-focused leadership seemed at times to be incongruent with the nature of our mission. I can personally attest, however, to the fact that it was exactly what the new college graduates (our students) and her instructors (myself and my peers) needed most. We felt valued and would have done anything for her personally or for the organization.

People desperately want to be heard; they crave meaningful leadership[221] that takes their feelings and opinions into account. Empathy is the secret sauce that allows leaders to meet their goals while simultaneously caring for those they lead.[222] A servant leader like Marné Deranger works hard to understand and empathize with others,[223] feeling *with* their followers rather than feeling *for* them. Servant leaders are other-centered. They value people and are orientated toward empathy.[224]

> The hearing that is only in the ears is one thing.
> The hearing of the understanding is
> another.

---

[221] Kriger and Seng 2005.
[222] Stefano and Wasylyshyn 2005, p. 6.
[223] Spears 2010, p. 27.
[224] Matteson and Irving 2006.

But the hearing of the spirit is not limited to any
one faculty, to the ear, or to the mind.
Hence it demands the emptiness of all the faculties.
And when the faculties are empty, then the
whole being listens.

There is then a direct grasp of what is right there before you that can never
be heard with the ear or understood with the mind.

—Chuang-Tzu[225]

Daniel Goleman[226] claims that emotional intelligence is a more important
determinant for success in management than technical expertise or cognitive
ability, and quantitative studies tend to agree.[227] Though empathy is a passive
trait, it can be learned. Leaders who are lucky enough to possess high EQ scores
still have to operationalize that trait when dealing with employees. Empathy
accounted for 20 percent of the positive variance in leadership scores in the
1954 Bell and Hall Jr. study.[228] Leaders who demonstrate empathy are more
likely to be perceived as successful by their peers.[229]

If you can learn a simple trick, Scout, you'll get
along a lot better with all kinds of folks.
You never really understand a person until you consider things from his
point of view, until you climb inside of his skin and walk around in it.
—Atticus Finch in *To Kill a Mockingbird*

Teaching empathy to someone who has not demonstrated an innate ability to
be empathic can be a difficult, if not impossible, task. There is a major roadblock
you encounter when trying to teach someone to be an empathetic leader.

AUTHENTICITY.

---

225 Found in: Rosenberg 2015.
226 Goleman 1995.
227 Chen and Jacobs 1997.
228 Bell and Hall Jr. 1954.
229 Kellett, Humphrey, and Sleeth 2006.

If you have to teach someone to understand the feelings of another, how authentic can their transformation be? If they were not empathetic before, can their empathy be believed? Is there congruence between their previously held and currently held beliefs, words, and actions? If a leader has not behaved with empathy before, then it might be difficult for anyone to believe that empathy is an authentically held belief on their part.

Emotion, learning, and leading are inextricable phenomenon. The lack of professional discourse regarding emotion is damaging the formation of trusting relationships, especially in leadership development. It is unclear why these invaluable social skills are not the focus of more management trainings. Maintaining focus on the other while remaining open to authentic emotional relationships is necessary and meaningful in both a professional and personal sense.

Perhaps the education to become a leader is more appropriately addressed in a department of philosophy setting than a business school setting. There is a marked difference between leaders and managers. A business program has a necessary focus on accounting and finance. These skills are necessary for running a business, but the temptation to equate a person with a number may be greater for a financier than for a philosopher. The focus in an arts and science program on liberal studies means that a more holistic approach is favored. Leadership should emerge as a natural and holistic function of personhood.

> It is not enough to know that they see things differently.
> If you want to influence them, you need also to understand
> empathetically the power of their point of view and to feel
> the emotional force with which they believe in it.
> —William Ury[230]

Authentic emotions come from the individual. These emotions are unsolicited and are based on in-the-moment reactions. That is not to say that they are untempered. Authentic emotions can be predetermined based on a disciplined understanding and mental models built on experience dealing with such emotions.

> You have power over your mind—not outside events.

---

[230] Cofounder of the Harvard Program on Negotiation and the International Negotiation Network with former president Jimmy Carter.

Realize this, and you will find strength.

—Marcus Aurelius

Avoid narcissism like the plague. If you start to feel your ego getting out of check, find your mentor or grab a moment of stillness for critical reflection. Empathy has no greater enemy than self-absorption.[231] Leadership is about others. Focusing on yourself contracts your worldview so you can no longer see past the end of your nose. Thinking of others first lends us the perspective that is so valuable to a leader. Perspective allows us to see the world as it is, absent petty self-absorption. Your world expands when you focus on others. You are more able to connect, to empathize compassionately when you are not at the center of your own universe.

> These are leaders who are highly ambitious for the greater good. And because they're ambitious for a greater good, they feel no need to inflate their own egos. And they, according to the research, make the best business leaders. And if you look at these qualities in the context of compassion, we find that the cognitive and affective components of compassion—understanding people and empathizing with people—inhibits, tones down, what I call the excessive self-obsession that's in us, therefore creating the conditions for humility. (Chade-Meng Tan[232])

An amusing article on leadership by Lt. Colonel Dan Ward talks about two views of the iconic villain Lord Darth Vader (from *Star Wars*). One person described him as a tyrannical figure who commands obedience, while another said he was authoritative and commanded respect.[233] The distinction between maniacal dictators and servant leaders, among other differences, is their motivation.[234] Servant leaders pursue their vision from a place of humility, empathy, and ethical behavior—a model that is follower-centric, ennobling, and enabling.

Not to carry the Darth Vader analogy too far, but patience is something that should be practiced not only with yourself but with your subordinates. Some of you probably remember the scene in *The Empire Strikes Back* where

---

[231] Goleman 2006.
[232] Tan 2010.
[233] Ward 2011.
[234] Lad and Luechauer 1998.

Admiral Ozzel gets Force choked by Darth Vader for coming out of light speed too late. He was in command of the task force that was to root the Rebel Alliance out of its secret base on Hoth. His reversion to realspace too close to the system alerted the Rebels to the Imperial presence, allowing them time to mount a defense. His decision was a simple miscalculation. It was a decision that should have been well within the scope of an admiral's practice, but that didn't matter to Darth Vader. In front of another subordinate, he calls Admiral Ozzell *clumsy* and *stupid*, attacking his character, rather than his action. Vader immediately calls the admiral and chokes him to death in full view of the bridge crew of the Star Destroyer.

It goes without saying that this is an extreme case of lacking empathy and patience. The illustrative nature of the event cannot be undervalued, however. As Darth Vader did not listen to his subordinates, as he failed to exercise patience with failure, managers often fail to allow their subordinates the freedom to fail. As leaders, we serve others. We allow that others will occasionally make mistakes. We are there for our followers when mistakes are made, not necessarily to punish but to guide.

> Treating employees benevolently shouldn't be viewed as an added cost that cuts into profits, but as a powerful energizer that can grow the enterprise into something far greater than one leader could envision.
> —Howard Schultz

Guidance after a mistake is made means that you must forgive the offense. A difficult conversation has to happen between you and the person who made the error. The conversation will be uncomfortable for you because you have the obligation to point out the error. It will be embarrassing for the employee because they have to admit fault, repent, and ask for another chance. It is up to you to decide how to respond. When the nature of the mistake allows, choose to err on the side of kindness. The situation has to allow for forgiveness, however. If forgiving the mistake would cause you, as a leader, to make an ethically unsound choice, then forgiveness is not an option.

When a mistake is made, a confrontation is necessary. In the same way that leaders must hold themselves accountable, never making excuses for mistakes, they are also responsible for holding their followers accountable.

PEOPLE DESERVE COMPASSION AND FORGIVENESS.

Never criticize the character of a follower in the presence of other followers. You undercut their future effectiveness and teach those below you that you are not to be trusted. The ripple effects of your lack of patience serves to destroy your organization from within. It is a pervasive rot that will eventually lead to a complete lack of trust in leadership.

Practice affirmation. Never seek to negate, offer quick solutions for, or otherwise question the feelings of your subordinates. People all have things going on in their lives. In addition to personalities and behaviors, people are shaped by their recent past. A person's attitude is often altered based on the events that have happened to them in the last few hours or days. Empathy requires inclusivity.

When Living Your Leadership, we always strive for inclusivity. Criticism is futile and dangerous.[235] It is unlikely that a critical leader will ever inspire their followers to achieve. Inspiration depends on the leader believing and accepting the follower for who they are. Larry Spears suggests that empathy in servant leadership practice involves assuming the best intentions of coworkers, valuing their inherent worth as humans while still holding people to standards of behavior.[236]

> Whoever you are, bear in mind that appearance is not reality. Some people act like extroverts, but the effort costs them energy, authenticity, and even physical health. Others seem aloof or self-contained, but their inner landscapes are rich and full of drama. So the next time you see a person with a composed face and a soft voice, remember that inside her mind she might be solving an equation, composing a sonnet, designing a hat. She might, that is, be deploying the powers of quiet. (Susan Cain[237])

---

[235] Carnegie 1998.
[236] 2005.
[237] 2012, p. 266.

CHAPTER RECAP

Empathy is a key component in leadership. A leader must strive to understand, to put themselves in another's shoes, and put that understanding to good use.

- Empathy can be learned, but empathy should never be inauthentic.
- Leadership depends on other-focus. Narcissism is antithetical to the practice of Living Your Leadership.
- Patience and forgiveness are skills that must be mastered for empathy to thrive.
- Affirm the feelings of your subordinates. You do not have to personally feel them or understand the emotions they experience, but that does not invalidate their authenticity.

LIVE AUTHENTICALLY

Being who we are requires that we can talk openly about things
that are important to us, that we take a clear position on where we
stand on important emotional issues, and that we clarify the limits
of what is acceptable and tolerable to us in a relationship.

—Harriet Lerner[238]

Authentic leadership has been shaped in the public consciousness in the
last two decades by some of the earliest popular management literature by
Bill George[239] in his book *Authentic Leadership: Rediscovering the Secrets to
Creating Lasting Value.* Self-actualization, the path to self-awareness, is not to
be trivialized. You cannot be expected to complete the journey in any specific
time frame. An authentic leader is self-aware, and with that awareness comes
the understanding that self-actualization is a journey, though authentic leaders
are often described as being self-actualized.[240]

Give me beauty in the inward soul;
may the outward and inward man be at one.

—Socrates

As an authentic leader, self-awareness and self-regulation are necessary

---

[238] Dr. Lerner is a clinical psychologist and a major contributor to feminist theory and therapy.

[239] George 2003.

[240] Kruse 2013.

attributes.[241] Self-awareness, the knowledge of strengths, weaknesses, and emotions, is a necessary precursor to being able to act in a truly transparent and genuine manner. Transparency necessitates sameness in behavior in public and in private.[242]

Authentic self-regulation processes:[243]

1. Internalized regulatory system driven by the leader's intrinsic self
2. Unbiased processing of self-related information
3. Actions that reflect self-core values
4. Relational transparency

The crucial aspect of authenticity as it pertains to Living Your Leadership is how others perceive the congruity of a leader's behavior with their purported values, their *true self*.[244] Authenticity cannot be developed except in community, in a dialogue,[245] not in isolation. The perception of others may not always be accurate or fair[246] in their assessment of your qualities or behavior as a leader, but developing patience and consistently showing yourself to be as you wish to seem[247] will pay dividends in the perception of your leadership over time.

Dialogue is a necessary part of developing leadership authenticity. I am not in full accord with Berkovich[248] when he asserts that it is not possible to develop authentic potential through study and critical reflection. His point is that looking back retrospectively can lead to self-deception, a common cognitive bias. It makes sense that a person would want to cast themselves in the best light possible, but that sort of self-deception runs counter to the correct application of critical reflection. Exploring your own values, beliefs, and priorities is a necessary first step to developing your authenticity in dialogue with others.

Though authenticity can be developed through reflection and study, leadership is a social process. The circle of dialogical pedagogy[249] is a brilliant self-reinforcing tool to better understand how authenticity is developed in community.

---

[241] Gardner, Avolio, and Walumbwa 2005.
[242] Albion 2006.
[243] Berkovich 2014.
[244] Kernis and Goldman 2006.
[245] Berkovich 2014.
[246] Johnson 2003.
[247] Socrates.
[248] Berkovich 2014, p. 246.
[249] Figure 13.

Genuine Dialogue

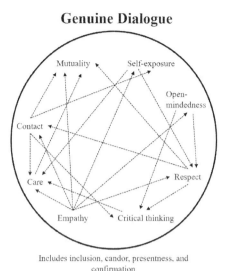

Includes inclusion, candor, presentness, and
confirmation

Figure 13. The circle of dialogical pedagogy[250]

Before attempting to practice authentic leadership, a leader should first develop themselves in accordance with self-leadership theory. It is not possible to be authentic if you don't know who you are as a person—if you don't recognize your strengths and flaws. You must be willing to pursue a path of authenticity that is, above all, internally and externally congruent. Once you know yourself, it is then possible to proceed to the external practice of your leadership.

> The privilege of a lifetime is to become who you truly are.
> —C. G. Jung[251]

Though authentic leadership is a practice, the focus should not be solely on externally visible actions but also on your self-narrative. Authenticity requires the alignment of your thoughts and actions in practice.[252] It is not only your personally held beliefs regarding your leadership and moral nature.

---

[250] Berkovich 2014, p. 252.
[251] Carl Gustav Jung (1875–1961), a Swiss psychiatrist and psychoanalyst credited with founding analytical psychology.
[252] Kouzes and Posner 1989.

Actions that align with your internally held beliefs are of critical importance to your followers.

> To be nobody but myself
> - in a world which is doing its best, night and
> day, to make me somebody else -
> means to fight the hardest battle any human
> can fight, and never stop fighting.
> —e. e. cummings

Aligned actions will ensure that the image you are projecting is the image that is real. A leader should *be* as they wish to *seem*; *be* is meant to be an active verb. Living Your Leadership is a practice that should be exercised in the open. As General George S. Patton wrote to his son, "You are always on parade." Transparent practice informs who you are as a person and leader, meaning that Living Your Leadership requires action, but it is more than just action;[253] it is who you are.

Putting authenticity into practice starts with critical self-examination. Through self-knowledge, a leader will gain an understanding of their strengths, weaknesses, character, and flaws. Without a critical understanding of self, it is not possible to be the best version of yourself. That is of primary utility. Books like these, training programs, and life experiences must be incorporated and viewed through the lens of critical self-reflection in order for authentic self-improvement to occur.

> When you are living the best version of yourself, you inspire
> others to live the best versions of themselves.
> —Steve Maraboli[254]

Authenticity is not something that you *are* until it is something that you *practice*. Being authentic is a useful skill only if you are acting as the best version of yourself. Some people mistake authentic leadership for just coming out and being who they are in any given situation. What if that person is an asshole? An inauthentic leader will demean, intimidate, exploit, criticize, and belittle their followers,[255] but an authentically mean leader will do the same. Authentic leadership requires that a leader be the best version of themselves.

---

[253] Cashman 2008.

[254] Dr. Maraboli is a behavioral scientist. He writes and speaks extensively on motivational psychology, leadership dynamics, and the peak performance mind-set.

[255] Sutton 2007.

Authenticity is a collection of choices that we have to make every day.
It's about the choice to show up and be real.
The choice to be honest.
The choice to let our true selves be seen.

—Brené Brown

Authentic servant leadership relies on the understanding that a leader is primarily concerned not with themselves but with others. An authentic, transformational leader creates trust through transparency; they communicate and share with others.[256] They display loyalty and recognize and reward their followers.[257] Through delegation and collaboration, they empower their followers while maintaining a positive relationship that allows for scaffolding to occur, acting as coach and mentor.

Effective authentic practice can be gauged. This is not something that is often talked about in literature. Measuring authenticity requires soliciting feedback. Who knows you? Not just who do you talk to on a daily basis, or who do you go drinking with at the bars at night, or who was your childhood best friend. Who intimately knows your character? Who knows what you behave like when the chips are down? On the flipside, who knows what you are like at your best? Who knows what you are capable of when you put your mind to it? And this is very important: who has been around to see you over a span of time? Two easily avoidable leadership assessment mistakes that are all too common are as follows: (1) attempting to judge the effectiveness of our authentic practice ourselves without going through the discernment of critical reflection and (2) asking someone who we have not known over time.

> The purpose of life seems to be to acquaint a man with himself and whatever science or art or course of action he engages in reacts upon and illuminates the recesses of his own mind. Thus friends seem to be only mirrors to draw out and explain to us ourselves; and that which draws us nearer our fellow man, is, that the deep Heart in one, answers the deep Heart in another,—that we find we have (a common Nature)—one life which runs through all individuals, and which is indeed Divine. (Ralph Waldo Emerson)

---

[256] Gottlieb and Sanzgiri 1996.
[257] Huber 2007.

Just like life itself, leadership is a journey. It is not a destination. You do not suddenly arrive at an understanding of yourself and start behaving as an authentic servant leader from that point forward. You are improving or backsliding all the time.[258] No one ever promised that the journey toward leadership excellence would be easy. It does not matter that you followed a formulaic approach. It does not matter that you read this or any other book. There will be setbacks. It takes perseverance to succeed in your personal struggle. Since we are in a constant state of change, we need to have someone who can judge the way we were versus the way we are—a friend, a mentor, a trusted family member.

Organizations have started to figure out limited ways of taking a snapshot of the whole person. By instituting measures like 360-degree leadership measurement, organizations are able to ascertain some of the strengths and weaknesses that their employees have, based on guidance from subordinates, peers, and superiors. Though this approach is a snapshot in time and relies on preformatted questions for each person to answer, it is an invaluable tool for the person receiving the feedback. Gaining an understanding of what people at any level think of you, comparing and contrasting their opinions, and incorporating that understanding into your leadership practice allows you to present a unified, authentic image of who you are.

It is easy to relapse into old patterns of behavior if profound change has not been internalized. Consequently, follow-up is absolutely necessary. Follow-up should be accomplished at regular intervals in order to ensure compliance with internal expectations. Talk to your friend, the person you have chosen to hold you accountable to the change you are trying to make. Ask them to check in with you on your authenticity practice progress.

A leader should be both who they are *and* who they want to be at all times. They are not defined or limited by the positions they are in or the rank that they hold. Are you a frontline manager? Are you a director? Are you an executive? Does any of that matter in the way you behave? Do you think a certain job title will automatically make you a better leader?

Your *decisions* define your leadership. As your choices define you, those choices that are visible to others define your leadership in their eyes. As you do the hard work to achieve congruence between your values and actions, you will be surprised how resilient, effective, and energized you can be![259]

---

[258] Algera and Lips-Wiersma 2012.
[259] Cashman 2008.

> Your words and deeds must match if you expect
> employees to trust in your leadership.
> —Kevin Kruse[260]

Regardless of the situation, whether you are in a high-stress job, a combat situation, a teaching position, or a mid- to high-level civilian job, you should be who you always strive to be. Your actions should demonstrate that you care for your people first.

If you change your behavior with your situation or with your position, you are inauthentic. Anyone who has known you through that transition will become suspicious of you as a leader and as a person (and rightly so!). Those who you lead will be able to recognize the change and will resent you for it and be suspicious of your motives.

> Leadership is not about personality, possessions, or charisma,
> but all about who you are as a person.
> I used to believe that leadership was about style
> but now I know that leadership is about substance, namely character.
> —James C. Hunter[261]

What others see to be true is, in the final calculation, what is truth to them. Our authentic practice must, therefore, be entirely visible to our followers. If the perceptions of others are such a large part of what makes or breaks our authentic leadership practice, it follows that understanding others in an empathetic way is a necessity. Once we are able to determine how we are perceived by others, we are better able to shape their perceptions based on a change in our behavior.

It is easy to slide into manipulative behavior using this method. Manipulation of others is *not* a desirable leadership attribute. *Leadership is influence*, according to John Maxwell. As leaders, it is our responsibility to ensure that manipulation does not wear the deceptive shroud of influence.

AUTHENTICITY DEMANDS INTEGRITY.

Rather than thinking of the conscious change in behavior on your part as a manipulation of others, think of it as bringing into alignment their *perceptions*

---

[260] Founder and CEO at LEADx.org, best-selling author and entrepreneur.

[261] Internationally best-selling author on servant leadership.

and your *intentions*. As long as your behavior imitates your internal intentions and is aligned with your dynamic lens of self-knowledge, you can rest assured that you are not falling into a pattern of hypocrisy. Acting in such a way that your behavior is perceived in the same way as you intended it to have been perceived, the image you project to others will be more effective and authentic.

> The honesty of authenticity, projecting your true self, and being vulnerable to the criticism and view of others requires that you reject the idea of shame for your actions. So often in business we think that a very proper and stern way of conducting ourselves as 'know-it-alls' and macho men and women is the way to be. But I actually believe that business is built on relationships. Relationships are built on trust and trust is built on vulnerability and transparency. (Marcus Lemonis[262])

---

[262] Serial entrepreneur, investor, CEO of Camping World, and star of CNBC's *The Profit*.

CHAPTER RECAP

Authentic leaders are self-aware; their actions are aligned with a deep understanding of self. They embrace self-regulatory behaviors as part of their practice of authenticity.

- Leadership is a social process that involves genuine dialogue.
- Authenticity does not imply a life lived solely for the consumption of others. A leader reflects on their personally held beliefs and acts in accordance with them; their actions are not just for show.
- If you want to measure authenticity, ask a close friend or associate, someone who knows you well.
- Authentic practice requires time to develop. Authenticity is built on the decisions you make and the actions you take.
- An authentic leader does not manipulate their followers. Their actions must mirror their internal intentions and closely held beliefs.

CONTROL AND AUTONOMY

You can't serve if you try to control the people you serve ...
—Michael Gates Gill[263]

Seventh-floor storage was a mess. I had volunteered to lead the process improvement effort to implement a 6S program[264] in order to increase the functionality and efficiency of the clinical technology workspace at my hospital. I had no idea that seventh-floor storage even existed until my lead engineer, Craig, walked me up there one day with a smirk on his face.

Like many things in a large organization with a lot of history, there are nooks and crannies just waiting to be discovered. Seventh-floor storage had existed in its state of miserable disarray for years. To give you an idea of the unusually large space, it was about forty feet long and fifteen feet wide, with twenty-foot-high ceilings. Initially, I was really excited to learn that we had additional storage that I didn't know about. Once we got to the room, however, I learned the reason that my lead engineer was chuckling to himself.

I had established the reputation of being enthusiastic, verbally espousing the tenets of servant leadership. This was my first real position out of the military, and I was excited and enthusiastic about doing the best I could. I worked closely with my subordinates and superiors and kept the lines of

---

[263] 2008, p. 176.

[264] 5S derives from the five Japanese words that make up the stages of 5S. Each word starts with the letter S. 6S adds the additional S, representing safety. For more information: https://www.epa.gov/sites/production/files/2015-06/documents/module_5_6s.pdf.

communication open to my dotted-line on site and my superiors at regional headquarters.

A man named Carlos was my first supervisor after the military. He was an air force veteran and had worked in the biomed field for over thirty years. I had a great deal of respect for Carlos. He had often talked about the value that he placed on mentorship as a primary quality of leadership practice.

Back to the seventh floor. Our storage was located on a patient-care floor dealing primarily with high-acuity, telemetry patients. The other end of the floor had space for staging areas and bed storage. As Craig and I stood in front of the door, I remarked how strange it was that we had such a large space dedicated to our equipment, especially since our main shop space was so small. He just laughed at me and said, "Just wait 'til you see it, Chris."

He punched in the combination and opened the door … into pure chaos. The door only cracked open about six inches before it hit an obstruction. Craig pushed a little harder and was able to get it open just enough for us to slide into the room. It was packed floor to ceiling, back to front, side to side with medical equipment, refuse, and old supplies. I had never seen anything like it in my professional life. I remember opening the shipping containers in Iraq when we received updated equipment and how it was typically labelled and categorized. The contrast was stark.

I'm not ashamed to admit that it was an exciting discovery for me. I have a true bias toward action, and I love to take on opportunities that will allow me to get my hands dirty. By the time I got back to my office, I had a plan in mind. I called Carlos and told him about the situation. I described the process of 6S and told him that I needed some managerial latitude in order to make decisions that might not be incredibly popular. He happily agreed, seeing an opportunity for one of his new hires to make a real difference.

Carlos gave me the autonomy I needed to gradually empty that room and make sure that all of the pieces of equipment were disposed of, put back in use, or properly organized. That is one of the most efficient and useful spaces in the region now with enough room to store anything needed for a major technology initiative. We saved thousands of dollars by putting equipment back in service alone! I can't imagine how difficult that process would have been, how demotivated I would have been, had I not had the support and autonomy granted by Carlos.

Employees who feel a natural, internal inclination to do what they are asked to do are more likely to perform well. This is a truism you do not have to search far to find proof of. This does not mean that, as the leader, you do not have the responsibility to direct work. That is absurd.

One of the key behaviors that determine your effectiveness as an inspirational leader is finding a way to motivate employees to do something that is meaningful to them and aligns with the organizational mission. Intrinsically motivated employees will continue to perform long after any external incentives have been exhausted. An intrinsically motivated follower is a highly desirable organizational asset because they embody the internal alignment of organizational goals.

Intrinsic motivation involves performing an action based on your desire to do so, rather than external pressure or incentive.

Locus of causality[265] sounds intensely academic. It is not as complex as it seems. Locus of causality refers to the perceived source of a behavior or attitude. For example, when an individual is offered a reward for performing to a specific standard, that individual will begin to perform the task in order to receive the reward, not because of any native interest.

Having an internal locus of causality simply means that you are acting based on your own desire to do so. You are predisposed to perform the action because what you are doing is aligned with your goals or your passions. Intrinsically motivated action is longer lasting and produces positive mental models about work.

This is crucial for leaders to understand. People motivated to do their jobs just for the money are typically not as happy as those who do something that they love. As the locus of the motivational orientation moves from internal to external on the continuum,[266] it is detrimental to a person's self-worth.[267] An intrinsically motivated person's locus of control is internal. That person will work harder because they want to, not because they are being controlled.[268, 269, 270, 271]

Choice plays a crucial role in self-determination. When a person has the ability to choose and they are also highly intrinsically motivated, they will achieve great results![272] Would you be motivated to put forth your best effort if you did not have a choice but to do what you were told? What if you were forced to complete a task that you were not interested in doing in the first place? For most people, the answer is simple: they would be less intrinsically motivated

[265] Figure 14.
[266] See figure 14.
[267] Deci, Connell, and Ryan 1989.
[268] Burton, Lydon, D"Alessandro, and Koestner 2006.
[269] Cameron, Pierce, Banko, and Gear 2005.
[270] Cordova and Lepper 1996.
[271] Deci and Ryan 1985.
[272] Ewing 2011.

to perform the task well. Even if people are offered extrinsic rewards, they are less likely to perform well if they do not have a choice in their task assignment.

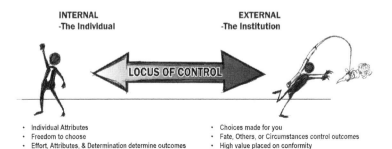

Figure 14. Locus of control continuum

For many leaders, it is almost instinctual to tighten control to increase efficiency. People are naturally inclined to manage by exception. This is an anachronistic view of the all-encompassing bureaucratic organization. How many Dilbert[273] cartoons have been drawn about the pointy-haired boss attempting to control his subordinates? The counterintuitive truth is that investing authority in your followers, allowing them autonomy, will pay dividends in innovation and work ethic.[274]

Leaders who control their followers, rather than trusting them by delegating, are ignoring the benefits of intrinsic motivation and high follower self-efficacy beliefs. Control decreases autonomy, which in turn negatively affects intrinsic motivation.[275] Autonomous followers feel competent[276] because they are trusted by their leaders.

Competency beliefs are enhanced when a person believes that their behavior is self-directed or highly internal.[277] Pursuing a transformational leadership style that values the development of employees increases intrinsic motivation.[278] Individualized consideration[279] reaffirms their value both as

---

[273] Comic strips by Scott Adams known for satirical office humor about a white-collar, micromanaged engineer, Dilbert.

[274] Amar 2009, p. 22.

[275] Vadell and Ewing 2011.

[276] de Charms 1968.

[277] Ryan and Deci 2000.

[278] Spears 2010.

[279] Bass 1998.

people and to the organization. As the individualized consideration[280] is applied, employees feel empowered to make a positive impact based on their performance,[281] shifting their locus of control in an internal direction.[282]

Transformational leadership is described as a process that motivates people by appealing to higher ideas and moral values, defining and articulating a vision of the future and forming a base of credibility.[283] The transformational leader looks to the future, understanding the need for change and how to bring such understanding to followers.

As they envision the future, transformational leaders see opportunities and are likely to proactively pursue them. A positive orientation toward change is a common attribute of the transformational leader.[284] Two commonly agreed-upon characteristics of the transformational leader are (1) questioning assumptions and promoting nontraditional thinking and (2) developing their followers.[285, 286]

In today's ever-changing global information economy, the transformational leader will be the one to bring it all together. They work to change from the inside out, focusing on the process but not failing to remember the people involved. An organization seeking change needs transformational leaders to motivate and guide employees toward the organizational goal.[287]

Table 2. Qualities of transformational leadership styles

Idealized attributes / Influence (transformational)	Leaders are seen as respected, trusted role models; they can be counted on and demonstrate high moral and ethical standards.
Inspirational motivation (transformational)	Leader's behavior motivates and inspires followers; team spirit is aroused; enthusiasm and optimism are displayed; and both leaders and followers create positive visions of the future.

---

[280] See table 2.
[281] Sendjaya and Sarros 2002.
[282] Rotter 1966.
[283] Tracey and Hinkin 1998.
[284] Crant and Bateman 2000.
[285] Tracey and Hinkin 1998.
[286] Bass and Avolio 1994.
[287] Tucker and Russell 2004.

Intellectual stimulation (transformational)	Leaders stimulate and encourage innovation, creativity, and questioning of old assumptions. New ideas are welcomed, and there should be no fear of mistakes or going against the grain.
Idealized attributes, idealized behaviors, inspirational motivation, and intellectual stimulation constitute *transformational leadership*.	
Individualized consideration (transformational)	Special attention is paid to each individual's needs and differences. Effective listening and developing of potential and personalized interaction are all components of this leadership style.
Individualized consideration is the transformational half of a *developmental exchange*.	

Sources: Bass and Avolio 1994; Bass 1998; Avolio et al. 1999; Parry and Proctor-Thomson 2002.

In much the same way that prisoners become institutionalized, lowering the chance of success in their eventual transition to freedom, leaders who make their followers dependent are doing those followers a serious disservice. Any system that robs individuals of their liberty in exchange for convenience is guilty of perpetuating a cycle of dependence. It is a cycle that ultimately results in behavior that is characterized by an inability to function outside that system.

As employees act more like automatons, as opposed to autonomous individuals, they are less likely to produce exceptional results. You have started treating them like machines. Like machines, employees who do not have autonomy will perform to standard, no more. It is not uncommon for a charismatic leader to fall into the same pattern as a narcissistic or controlling leader, micromanaging their followers. The trap here is subtler, however. In the case of a charismatic leader, followers may choose emotional dependence voluntarily based on their feelings of attachment to the leader.

Emotional dependence is a direct result of a shift in the locus of causality from the individual to the system. Howell and Avolio conducted a study of seventy-eight managers that indicated a correlation between transformational leadership behaviors and higher internal locus of control. It showed that transactional behaviors resulted in poor business unit performance.[288] Transactional leaders focus on the stick-and-carrot approach to leading, using money or threats or other external levers to control their employees.

A leader, using emotionally abusive tactics, can cause emotional dependence, but they can just as easily do so by providing too much for

---

[288] Howell and Avolio 1993.

subordinates. Followers will inevitably have lower self-efficacy beliefs if they do not have mastery experiences to influence their self-talk.[289] When those subordinates do not feel that they are capable, they are less likely to take initiative when confronted with novel situations.

MICROMANAGING IS A SYMPTOM OF ARROGANCE.[290]

Often a leader will choose to focus on the process to the exclusion of the big picture. Micromanaging threatens a subordinate's perceived self by calling into question their ability to perform their job in an effective, self-directed manner. It irrevocably retards their progress toward becoming self-actualizing[291] individual contributors. When employees feel controlled, they are demotivated.[292] When a follower is crushed under an oppressive manager, it removes their sense of agency; their locus of control is shifted away from themselves and toward the organization. Leaders who provide their employees with the autonomy to create value are encouraging the development of self-determination.[293]

> We are called to live not as one without others, above or against others,
> but with and for others.
> —Pope Francis

Turn your focus toward behaviors. Behaviors are the physical manifestation of a leader's beliefs and values.

While Living Your Leadership, it is critical to consider stressing behaviors over goals in organizational personnel assessments. One of the fatal flaws encountered in most corporations that employ yearly evaluations and annual performance reviews is to place too much weight on the goals section of the document. There is often a disproportionately large weight given for the goals section. The goals section is quantifiable and objective based. The behavioral section is composed of the soft skills that managers are required to display on a daily basis.

Goal setting and measurement is not inherently a bad thing. Individuals

---

[289] Figure 3.
[290] Cockerell 2008.
[291] Figure 6.
[292] Rockwell 2013.
[293] Den Hartog and Belschak 2012.

and organizations should have specific, measurable, actionable, and time-bound (SMART) goals against which to measure progress. The issue arises when those goals are pushed to the forefront at the expense of other competing concerns. The imbalance that is caused by focusing on business goals to the exclusion of more human concerns manifests itself in many ways.

The goals you find on yearly evaluations are obtained through a collective effort. In fact, often those goals are achieved through the efforts of hundreds or even thousands of people. Anyone taking responsibility for the work done on the front line is disingenuous at best.

You may have saved a few thousand dollars, but you certainly weren't responsible for hitting the efficiency goal that was calculated in the millions of dollars. In judging an individual on the goals achieved by the department during that year, there is an assumption that the individual was a necessary part of achieving each of those goals. This idea disregards at least one tenet of succession planning—that is, no individual is crucial to any organization; anyone is replaceable.

What separates driven and charismatic individuals who have succeeded from those who have failed? It is embodied in the behavioral section of the annual interview. Key behaviors include practicing humility, altruistic behavior, servant leadership, communication skills, accountability, and the list goes on and on.

Suppose you have a horribly egotistical manager, one who routinely chooses to exert authoritarian control and micromanages their staff. This manager still managed to achieve all of the department goals. Those goals are weighted at around 70 percent while behaviors are only 30 percent weight on an annual review. Even if they scored extremely low on all of the behavioral section, the lowest letter grade they could get is C-.

Despite a keen focus on the attainment of goals, employee and customer satisfaction scores are often strikingly negative. What is the leader sacrificing in order to achieve those goals? If the weighting of the goal section and the behavioral section are skewed too far toward the goals, the score derived from that evaluation would indicate to anyone glancing at it that goals matter more than behavior. If that is the case, your climate assessment will clearly reflect employee dissatisfaction.

You can whip a horse to a frenzy and beat all kinds of time records on the track, but the horse will suffer. Employees are not equine; though neither the horse nor the employee will benefit from literal or metaphorical whippings. They are human beings deserving of respect and dignity.

As leaders shift their focus to customers and quality, they realize that the old authoritarian leadership style does not work anymore. To achieve quality, service, and rapid response, leaders must utilize all available talent. They must find ways to inspire, involve, and empower employees. They must create a work environment that encourages commitment, innovation, and cooperation. Instead of evaluating, leaders now coach. Instead of doing, they delegate. Instead of telling, they facilitate. No one is expected to boss anyone. Everyone is expected to participate. (Dr. Suzanne Willis Zoglio[294])

Dictatorial leaders represent themselves as invaluable to the organization. Why wouldn't they, after all? The desire to control others is evidence of their own narcissism and an out-of-control ego. They revel in the measurable success that comes with attaining goals regardless of the expense levied on the backs of their employees.

The illustration of employee autonomy versus the exercise of management authority[295] indicates what happens to employees who are forced to serve under dictatorial leaders. Tyrannical leaders do not care about the morale or humanity of their subordinates. They care only what their bosses think of them. They think to themselves, *Who is paying my paycheck? What do they care about? Those people are below me for a reason. They exist solely to achieve the goals I am measured by.* The understanding of employees as beneath the leader is an example of vertical leadership and is the antithesis of a humble servant leader.

A servant leader realizes that they and their employees are part of a team. Their followers exist, for all intents and purposes, horizontal to them. Their staff are the most important people in the organization because they get the work done. The job of an authentic servant leader is to take care of their people. It is to clear the path for them and make sure they have the tools, time, and training necessary to get the job done efficiently and effectively.

All this talk about behaviors and goals may give the impression that behaviors are the end-all and be-all of an evaluative process. Organizational goals are not unimportant. That is an absurd idea. Measurable business success cannot be achieved without focusing on goals. The problem comes when the focus on goals overshadows attention that should be paid to the leadership

---

[294] *The Participative Leader,* p. 5.
[295] Figure 12.

behaviors. With autonomy supporting leadership, employees will want to work harder for intrinsic reasons. The result of that hard work will be faster and superior achievement of goals.

Using emotional intelligence and sound moral reasoning, the transformational leader is able to motivate others to achieve beyond expectations. Moral decision-making involves using ethical tools to determine the moral character of a decision. In most solid, ethical decision-making processes, the impact of a decision is also closely considered.

The relationship between transformational leadership and emotional intelligence is driven by conceptual overlap between their respective characteristics. The leader's personal, emotional, and social skills[296] and the personal, social, and emotional characteristics that make up EQ should be in alignment for a transformational leader to behave authentically.

Transformational-style leadership requires a certain level of political savvy. Political skill is the ability to leverage relationships in order to achieve organizational, team, and individual goals. Political skill is a capability that leaders must demonstrate daily.[297] There are four main practices for positive political skill:

1. Social awareness
2. Interpersonal influences
3. Networking
4. Sincerity

The use of political skill, like any other leadership behavior, must be used in an ethical way. The way a leader is perceived is mediated by the use of political skill. Conversely, political skill can be used to harm followers. It violates the respect a leader should have for their followers to influence them in a way that is unethical.

Misusing the influence that we have over others is the dark siren song of charismatic, transformational leadership. It should be noted that charismatic leadership is not transformational leadership[298] but is only part of the definition of transformational leadership as understood by the multifactor leadership questionnaire (MLQ) and other extant research.[299] Charisma is part of the *idealized influence* quality of transformational leadership.

---

[296] Bass and Avolio 1997.
[297] Ferris et al. 2005.
[298] Bass 1985.
[299] Bass and Steidlmeier 1999.

A fresh critical look is being taken at the issues of power and authority, and people are beginning to learn, however haltingly, to relate to one another in less coercive and more creatively supporting ways. A new moral principle is emerging, which holds that the only authority deserving one's allegiance is that which is freely and knowingly granted by the led to the leader in response to, and in proportion to, the clearly evident servant stature of the leader. (Robert Greenleaf[300])

---

[300] "Servant Leadership," p. 10.

CHAPTER RECAP

Intrinsic motivation does not rely on outside consequences or contingent rewards to enhance or maintain performance. An intrinsically motivated person performs because of an innate desire to accomplish a task.

- Encouraging intrinsic motivation in employees means that they will be happier and more productive in the long term.
- Giving your followers choices is motivating inasmuch as it cedes control from others to them.
- Controlling followers decreases autonomy, a crucial determinant in perceived self-direction.
- A further result of controlling employees over a period of time, micromanaging, is that employees will become used to behaving with external control determining their actions. This will preempt curiosity, initiative, and innovation.
- Behaviors are harder to measure, but they are what make up a person at work. Goals are typically a group effort and are less appropriate to weigh heavily in an annual evaluation.
- An emotionally intelligent leader considers the political and social ramifications of their words and deeds.

LEADING TEAMS

A person who is worthy of being a leader wants power
not for himself, but in order to be of service.
—Senator Sam J. Ervin Jr.

Focusing on the individual to the exclusion of the team constitutes a failure of vision. You are responsible for a high-performing *team*, not a group of individuals.[301] A team, working together, is greater than the sum of its parts. Leveraging team dynamics involves understanding the contributions of each individual to the group effort. Practicing transformational leadership behavior (e.g., servant leadership or mentoring) with individuals in your team adds value to the team and serves to encourage those individuals in their journey toward becoming intrinsically motivated leaders themselves.

While interviewing for my current position, I was asked, "In your experience, what is the key to developing a good team?" After a moment of thought, I replied, "The most important element in developing a functional team is building it on a foundation of trust." Several weeks later, one of my thirty-five-year union employees voiced during my first staff meeting that trust is something built through shared experience, and it can be broken much more readily than it can be earned. She asked, "Why should we trust you?"

It was a valid question at the time, since there had been a lot of internal bickering and management-versus-labor divisiveness in the past several years.

---

[301] Bennis 2007.

Standing there, confident in my experience and my knowledge but facing the inscrutable countenances of forty staff members, I was struck by the frustration and pain that they had experienced. I have made it a point to practice intentional reflection in my daily life, and today was no exception. I reflected on the promises that had been given to me and broken in my professional life. I thought about the book that I was writing (the one you are reading now) and the practices that I had been outlining in it.

It is not in my nature to spew management jargon. In attempting to build trust in a team setting, very little turns people off as quickly as hearing slick and seemingly disingenuous phrases like *leveraging capabilities* or creating *labor/ management synergy*. Trust is an emotional phenomenon[302] and should be viewed through a lens of empathy and nurtured through caring acts. How can you answer someone who asks why they should trust you, the leader, when she has had her trust broken by leaders in the past?

She had asked the question during the hour that I had scheduled for the round robin, a time for staff to question management about anything and everything in a nonattribution environment. This amount of time was purposefully excessive. With the level of distrust and dissatisfaction that the department had experienced in the recent past, it was important to me to air out the grievances so that we could identify and resolve them together. It was that context that gave me the answer I was looking for. I let her know that she should judge me by my actions.[303]

I reminded the team that we were spending this time together to get to know each other, to talk candidly about issues, and to develop plans to deal with them *in community*. In effect, I was taking the first step in the trust narrative: I was committing to a course of action based on the team's concerns.

Regardless of the state of the organization you lead, there are fundamental leadership traits that are crucial to ensuring an enduring leadership legacy. It is easy to take from those words that I mean your personal legacy of leadership within the department will live beyond your tenure. *That is not at all what I mean.* The leadership legacy can be carried on by any individual who embraces the *model* of leadership that you embodied during your tenure. A successful team requires a fundamental leadership strategy to endure.

Establishing trust among the team is a crucial step toward team cohesion. The stages of team development are forming, storming, norming, and performing.[304] In 1977, Bruce Tuckman and Mary Ann Jensen added

---

[302] Beatty and Brew 2004.
[303] See Matthew 7:15–20.
[304] Tuckman 1965.

adjourning to the model to indicate that groups complete tasks and come to a natural end.[305] Each stage of team development is necessary, and each will occur in any team, though not necessarily sequentially. The end state of the storming phase is trust amongst the members of the team. From there, establishing goals and vision, the more formulaic tasks can be attended to.

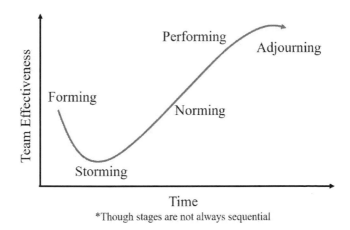

Figure 15. Tuckman's stages of group formation

Establishing trust is easier than people make it out to be. Reach out with your words and follow them with your actions. Do this consistently and over time.

TRUST IS BUILT ON FOLLOW-THROUGH.

The onus is on the leader to demonstrate the value of their word. A promise fulfilled by action is worth more than any clever turn of phrase or clichéd leadership saying. Follow-through is most often demonstrated after difficult conversations.

Followers need direction and guidance. Sometimes they need discipline or redirection. As a forward-thinking leader, you will have set expectations and communicate those expectations clearly. As projects mature, as group dynamics shift, there will be hiccups. As a leader, look out for those opportunities to gently but firmly confront issues as they arise.

---

[305] Tuckman and Jensen 1977.

Human resources at your organization may have a specific way they would prefer the interaction to take place, but the basic format is typically the same. You take your employee aside and speak to them candidly about the issue you have observed. Start with an opening statement that reminds the employee of the expectation you had set. Address the issue by focusing on the action that was taken, being careful to never criticize the personhood of the employee. Lay out your continued behavioral expectations and establish a plan to follow up that is time bound. Ask them if they have any questions or feedback for you.

From a continuous development and trust-building perspective, the most important action you can take is to follow up when you said you would. Make an appointment on your preferred work calendar. Jot a note in the calendar about the situation so that you are prepared for the conversation follow-up when it is time. Demonstrating that you care, that you are a person of integrity, will pay dividends in loyalty and personnel development down the road.

As you have read in the section on authenticity, the actions that you take as a leader should be transparent and perfectly aligned from your words to your actions. Transparency and integrity are key components of establishing trust in an organization because they are fundamental aspects of relationship building. Leadership revolves around relationships, and relationships are built on trust.

Establishing trust is the first step. There are so many moving pieces in an organization that it is easy to neglect building relationships. Trying to focus on each individual step outlined in a theory, to mechanically follow the formula you read in that ten-steps-to-better-leadership blog is unhelpful. Except in theory, leadership is not a linear process.

REAL LIFE IS MESSY, AND THAT IS OKAY.

Start from a place where you authentically practice servant leadership. There are always problems in our messy workplaces. Express sincere concern for your followers. Be genuine. Offer to help.

Leaders who exhibit individual-focused behavior across a group, paying attention and trying to focus on the individual needs of each team member, are practicing differentiated leadership.[306] Differentiated leadership means that a leader is trying to use various leadership styles for each person. They

---

[306] Wang and Howell 2010, p. 1135.

are employing leadership practices as if they were a tool in a tool chest, pulling out a wrench for some employees and a screwdriver for another.

Some models of leadership, like Full Range Leadership Development (FRLD),[307] employ valid techniques that must be memorized and incorporated into your practice. One of the issues with leadership paradigms like these is that the models require constant, directed thought to maintain the analysis and recommended action cycle. A leader is expected to assess, either based on the situation or the person being dealt with, what type of leadership behavior to adopt. If this is not performed with exquisite precision, it can easily be perceived as disingenuous behavior.

CARING FOR EACH MEMBER OF THE TEAM IS NECESSARY.

> Never lose sight of the fact that the most important yardstick
> of your success will be how you treat other people.
> —Barbara Bush

Treating them differently negatively impacts collective efficacy and group identification, simultaneously making it difficult for team members to know their leader in any authentic way. Living Your Leadership implies an intuitive use of the tools that are authentically yours. A leader is on display—transparent. Their techniques may differ based on need, but they are all connected to the core beliefs and self-leadership model built in the first half of this text.

Team members are people, deserving of respect regardless of their differences. The way to influence people and make that influence stick is through relationship building. High-quality relationships with your team members collectively[308] makes it more likely they will perceive your leadership as fair. Treating your employees as uniquely deserving of respect and human dignity will enhance team performance.[309] As a leader's influence impacts individual and team attitudes and values, team behaviors start to improve,[310] and culture starts to morph. If ignored by their leader, followers may not only deliver poor individual performance but may also undermine the performance of the team as a whole.[311]

---

[307] Stafford 2010.
[308] Wu, Tsui, and Kinicki 2010.
[309] Graen and Uhl-Bien 1995.
[310] Donohue and Wong 1994.
[311] Wang and Howell 2010, p. 1140.

THOSE THINGS THAT UNITE US ARE MORE PROFOUND THAN THOSE THAT DIVIDE US.

The generation gap is not as large or insurmountable as some people describe it to be. The Center for Creative Leadership has conducted an ongoing survey since March 2008[312] providing information on trends and issues related to generational cohorts. It has discovered the three generations, the boomers, Gen Xers, and millennials have more in common when it comes to the type of leadership that is most effective than is often speculated. All three generational cohorts agree on several characteristics of effective leaders: they participate and are team oriented, charismatic, and human oriented. Other relevant core attributes of an effective leader are having consideration for others, being able to inspire, having respect for those around them, and being able to excite others to do their very best.[313]

In a story told by Simon Sinek in his book *Start with Why*, he speaks about the American auto executives who visited a plant in Japan to learn more about their engineering process. Evidently, the Americans had employed individuals whose job was to tap car doors with a rubber mallet in order to make sure that they fit straight off the assembly line. There did not seem to be such a person employed in that activity in Japan. When the Japanese engineer tour guide was asked about this phenomenon, he replied that they designed the doors to fit during the engineering process and thus did not need to check it on the back end of the manufacturing process.

One of the truths that Mr. Sinek later mentions is that starting the thought process in a uniform manner, starting with why, allows us to align our teams, our vision, and our processes short term. Typically, reactive solutions are not necessary to correct anomalies in the process later when you start with why. If, as a leader, you start with a solid understanding of where you are going and engineer the process carefully by putting the right people in the right places, starting with *who* just as Jim Collins suggests, the need for motivation and inspiration is not necessary.

One of the air force's mantras is *flexibility is the key to airpower*. If you start with solid people, build processes, and work to ensure those processes are measured, continued, and repeated in the same formal and foresighted manner as when you started, you can be relatively assured that issues will not appear down the line unless there is external change. The need for flexibility in the

---

[312] Deal, Stawiski, Gentry, and Cullen 2013.
[313] Deal, Stawiski, Gentry, and Cullen 2013.

face of unanticipated change decreases to such an extent that questioning the reason why people need to be flexible in the first place seems absurd.

There are always things that are out of your control. The air force's motto about flexibility is not wrong. Hire the right people for the right jobs. Use foresighted strategical and tactical planning. Relying on the flexibility of your team is less efficient than designing an aligned process in the first place. Flexibility is almost always reactive in nature. It is great in a pinch, but expecting to rely on MacGyver-like skills[314] of your followers is shortsighted.

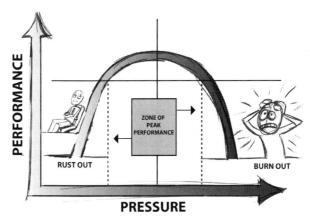

Figure 16. Yerkes-Dodson interpretation (replace *arousal* with *pressure*)[315]

You've read that, as a leader, you are always visible to your subordinates. Followers may have formed an opinion of you as a leader before you even take the formal role. They may have had expectations of anyone who holds the position you will be filling. Since that belief precedes your interaction with the team, it is necessary to consider how your first actions can garner trust and empower your team.

A self-aware leader realizes that the view of others in an organization directly impacts their leadership effectiveness. Initial actions set the tone for leadership tenure. Leaders should be sensitive to the reputational consequences

---

[314] An action-adventure TV series created by Lee David Zlotoff. MacGyver works for a clandestine organization and relies on his unconventional problem-solving skills in each episode to escape from harrowing situations and to save lives.

[315] The Yerkes-Dodson law describes an empirical relationship between arousal and performance. It was developed by psychologists Robert Yerkes and John Dodson in 1908.

that all of their decisions have,[316] most especially their first interactions with the team. You have taken over a team, but you have made mistakes.

Those mistakes do not have to define your tenure in the position or your leadership legacy. As an educated self-leader, you know that everyone makes mistakes. Working to overcome those missteps involves admitting fault, owning the consequences, and moving on. Your best is all that can ever be reasonably asked of you.

Empowering subordinates holds consequences for the way that others perceive your leadership. Suppose, for instance, that a leader delegates many important tasks to subordinates. Is the organizational culture such that their action would be viewed as weak? Would the typical employee or group of employees understand that delegation as a form of personal incompetence or would they see it as employee empowerment?

Surround yourself with the best people you can find, delegate authority, and don't interfere as long as the policy you've decided upon is being carried out.
—Ronald Reagan

The organizational setting is extremely important in examining the contextual effects of employee empowerment. The organizational setting can affect the way that subordinates perceive leadership attributes. It informs expectations of a leader and the level of empowerment that is appropriate. When a leader empowers their employees, it does not detract from the perceived stature of those leaders.[317] Rather, leaders who empower their employees are perceived to have higher-order leadership abilities than those who do not empower their employees.

Employee empowerment does not divest the leader of their accountability. A leader is ultimately accountable. The buck stops here. For example, if a change is directed at the organizational level, you are accountable for execution of the actions necessary for that change. You represent the organization and have the obligation to align your team's execution of policy change with the greater organization. When an employee asks, "Who directed this change?" as a prelude to questioning the wisdom of the effort, you should know what to say. As a leader who takes personal responsibility, you do not blame the situation on those who have authority over you.

A leader is one who knows the way, goes the way, and shows the way.

---

[316] Campbell and Campbell 2011.
[317] Campbell and Campbell 2011.

—John Maxwell

You own the change. That is not to say you do not have the obligation to challenge directives if they are unethical, immoral, or unlawful, however. With an understanding that the change is none of those things, you should exercise your personal responsibility and enthusiastically own the process.

There may be times that, as a leader, you agree with your subordinates regarding the unpopularity of a particular policy or directive from those above you. When I had to tell my flight that we were going to be participating in seventy-two-hour alerts, you can imagine that I was no happier than my people that I'd be spending that much time away from my family with no real return on that sacrifice. There are two avenues to approach negative change that will contribute to your leadership legacy: (1) authentically empathizing with your followers, listening to their concerns with empathy, and (2) soliciting ideas for improvements to the plan.

While you can always attempt to change your boss' mind, complaining to those you lead is never the answer.

AS A LEADER, YOU ARE ULTIMATELY ACCOUNTABLE.

As we move from the topic of team leadership to servant leadership, keep in mind that it is not one or the other but that Living Your Leadership is a unitary paradigm that encourages development from the inside out. The topics discussed in previous sections should be incorporated into the practices outlined in later sections so that the holistic nature of the paradigm can be realized. A leader is not judged as often by how they lead but by how they serve; value is achieved through service.[318]

---

[318] Cashman 2008.

CHAPTER RECAP

Leaders must lead themselves, focus on individuals, and realize that leadership endeavors involve a community of followers. Leading a team requires strategy and forethought, as well as carefully developed skill.

- Team development progresses in stages. The stages are not sequential but are all necessary.
- Trust is foundational to effective teams.
- Trust is established by follow-through and consistent feedback and guidance.
- Each member of a team should be treated with justice, fairly and consistently. Care for others should guide your decisions.
- Start with why, designing your processes for the end state.
- Leaders are always on display. They own their decisions, empower their followers, and embrace change.
- Ultimate accountability rests with a leader.

SERVANT LEADERSHIP

The servant-leader is servant first ... Becoming a servant-leader begins with the natural feeling that one wants to serve, to serve first. Then conscious choice brings one to aspire to lead. That person is sharply different from one who is leader first ... The difference manifests itself in the care taken by the servant first to make sure that other people's highest priority needs are being served. The best test, and the most difficult to administer, is this: Do those served grow as persons? Do they, while being served, become healthier, wiser, freer, more autonomous, more likely themselves to become servants?

—Robert Greenleaf

I got fired. It wasn't a proud day for me. I was finishing my dissertation and working sixty-hour weeks in a high-level position at my last air force base. My boss was a rabid micromanager and extremely uncommunicative. The man didn't take the time to actually give feedback on the work that I did. If he didn't like a detail of the speech I had spent hours writing, he would take the piece of paper it was written on, tear it halfway through, and leave it on my desk to find in the morning.

To be fair, I should have realized what I was getting myself into. He prominently displayed Machiavelli's *The Prince*[319] on his bookshelf and insisted

---

[319] Among the gems you can find in Machiavelli's work, these quotes stand in stark contrast to Living Your Leadership: "If an injury has to be done to a man it should be so severe that his vengeance need not be feared." "Never attempt to win by force what can be won by deception." "Since love and fear can hardly exist together, if we must choose between them, it is far safer to be feared than loved." And "He who wishes to be obeyed must know how to command."

on being called by his call sign (he wasn't a pilot and had never been to a combat zone but had *earned* his nickname in a school setting). On a day just like any other, I came into the office and learned that I had been reassigned.

Rather than being allowed to return to my previous position, I was forced into an operational job in a squadron run by one of that man's flunkies.

I decided to separate from active military service that day.

It was a bittersweet choice. The air force was my life. I had dedicated myself to the service and had excelled in every assignment, bar the last one. There was a lot of planning involved in choosing a civilian life. I had to find a job, figure out how to make the transition successful for my wife and two little boys, and move my family to a new location. In addition to the practical aspects of the transition, I had to deal with the emotional upheaval that my perceived failure had generated. Ultimately, I embraced the struggle.

Based on my solid performance as a junior officer, I was accepted by a firm that acts as a headhunter for companies nationwide looking for talented, experienced military leaders to serve in corporate America. During the hiring event, I was interviewed and chosen by Kaiser Permanente for a health care management position in Northern California.

Health care administration was the perfect crucible[320] for putting some of the tenets of self-sacrificial and servant leadership into practice.

Servant leadership (SL) is a large topic, and the characteristics of servant leaders are well defined.[321] It is a field of study that organizations like the Greenleaf Center[322] and the School of Business at Regent University[323] specialize in. This chapter is not meant to add to the scholarly research on the subject or to present a comprehensive review of the theory. Rather, it provides a practical overview of SL and how it applies in the Living Your Leadership practice.

> The highest of distinctions is service to others.
> —King George VI

Servant leadership derives from *agapao*, or sacrificial love.[324] Agapao is an ancient Greek term that describes charity as an unreciprocated loving action.

---

[320] De Pree 1989.

[321] Read about the ten characteristics of a servant leader from Spears 2010 at https://www.regent.edu/acad/global/publications/jvl/vol1_iss1/Spears_Final.pdf.

[322] https://www.greenleaf.org/.

[323] http://www.regent.edu/sbl/.

[324] Patterson 2003.

Not to be confused with transformational leadership, in which the leader's focus is on organizational goals and relies on charisma for power and influence, SL orients itself primarily on followers. Servant leaders show genuine interest in the lives of their followers.

A SERVANT LEADER UNABASHEDLY CARES.[325]

Though it may sound touchy-feely, loving your followers is a necessary part of leadership; it is an active investment in those you lead.[326] Many influential thought leaders have implied that a servant leader's motivation stems from their principles, values, and beliefs,[327] or from their humility and spiritual insights.[328] These very personal factors enable servant leaders to engage themselves in self-sacrificial,[329] altruistic behaviors.[330] A servant leader is a steward. A steward holds responsibility for an organization and followers in trust for future leaders. A good steward uses their time, talent, and treasure to provide for their followers in meaningful ways. The idea that one *serves* first, rather than *leads* first is a fundamental presupposition of servant leadership that distinguishes it from other models.[331]

A servant leader will attend to the needs of their followers. Their needs will preempt the needs of the organization.[332] This is a bifurcated process: (1) serving the needs of the followers and helping to reach their full potential and (2) inspiring them and maturing them to be leaders.[333] The servant style is designed to prepare followers for their own leadership journey. Mutual trust and empowerment are crucial for the servant-style leader to be successful.[334] Servant leaders empower their followers. They help followers grow and develop according to their needs and not at the whim of the organization. Power is ethically used, and teams work collaboratively and in an atmosphere of mutual respect and trust under an SL.[335]

---

[325] Crom 1998.
[326] Lorenz 2012.
[327] Farling, Stone, and Winston 1999.
[328] Graham 1991.
[329] Choi and Mai-Dalton 1998.
[330] Sendjaya and Sarros 2002.
[331] Sendjaya and Sarros 2002, p. 61.
[332] Howatson-Jones 2004.
[333] Greenleaf 1998.
[334] Spencer 2007.
[335] Greenleaf 1998.

Ye call me Master and Lord: and ye say well; for so I am.
If I then, your Lord and Master, have washed your feet;
ye also ought to wash one another's feet.
For I have given you an example,
that ye should do as I have done to you.
—John 13:13–15 KJV

As Robert Greenleaf famously said, the best test of SL success is whether "those served grow as persons; do they, while being served, become healthier, wiser, freer, more autonomous, more likely themselves to become servants?" One of the biggest problems with that particular statement is that employee growth toward a servant orientation is difficult to measure. It is not difficult to measure because tools do not exist to measure the phenomenon; it is difficult to measure because it requires an incubation period. Investing time in people is necessary in servant leadership.

Prioritize people over tasks.
—Cathy Engelbert[336]

It can sometimes take years before servant leadership takes full effect in those served. Robert Greenleaf understood this. As the head of the Servant Leader Institute (SLI) pointed out in his essay, servant leadership is a long-term transformational approach[337] and one that is holistic in nature, affecting both life and work.

There are practical and specific strategies for the implementation of servant leadership that move past the purely theoretical. Actually showing employees that you really care about each of them as people can take many forms. Here are a few to try on for size:

Learn the names of all of your people. This may seem basic, but it is important to recognize and use first names whenever possible because everyone matters.[338] If you are at all like me, it is extremely difficult for you to match faces with names. Something that I have done is to have pictures taken of all of my people and put their name underneath in order to memorize them on my own time. Try out some other tactics: when you are introduced, look at the person carefully and repeat their name in conversation several times. This tends to cause a link in your mind between the face and name.

---

[336] CEO at Deloitte, LLP.
[337] Spears 2005.
[338] Treasurer 2014.

Another tactic to show care for the individual is to ensure that you know something about each of your employees. What is important to them? Do they have a young family? Is one of the children about to graduate from college or high school? Are they foster parents? Do they compete in any sports or activities? Mention their personal details and follow up on important events.

Ensuring that you work with all of your people in the most respectful and personable manner means that they will be able to perceive that you care. They will know that you care about more than just getting the job done; you also care about the things that matter to them. An additional benefit is that you will be able to determine what kind of leadership direction your followers are most ready to accept. By this, I do not mean that you should change yourself to accommodate any one employee but that you should use a more or less authoritative style when dealing with certain individuals.

Here's a question to ask yourself: are you the most important person in the room? The answer to that question for any servant leader will *always* be no. Any and every person in that room is not only deserving of your respect, but their needs should be placed ahead of yours. This manifests itself in many ways. Perhaps you have been working on several initiatives that will affect your work unit. This has cost you an enormous amount of time and effort, but there were other people involved in the project that report to you. How you handle the success or failure of any of those initiatives shows those employees something about you as a leader.

The proponents of servant leadership set their practice in stark contrast to the traditional, autocratic, and hierarchical leadership styles. They emphasize that servant leadership involves cooperative decision-making, ethical behavior, and growth of the frontline worker. Many of the thinkers that you have been reading about in this book are proponents of either servant leadership, facilitative leadership, or some other form of leadership that does not tend to view workers as cogs in the industrial machine—thinkers like Robert Greenleaf, Stephen Covey, Max DePree, Ken Blanchard, and Jim Collins.[339]

Over the last fifteen years, SL has been expanding. The concept began with a person who wants to serve emerging into a leader. The servant leader style has spread across the world. The two words *servant* and *leader,* having opposite meanings, when joined describe an emerging paradox. Having a leader that serves their employees, helping to expand their knowledge and skills, is a radical concept. Thankfully, many organizations are moving toward this type of leadership style.

---

[339] Spears 2005.

I slept and dreamt that life was joy,
I awoke and saw that life was service,
I acted and behold, service was joy.
—Tagore[340]

The servant leader puts the needs of others before themselves. Greenleaf[341] described servant leadership as "[beginning] with the natural feeling that one wants to serve. Then conscious choice brings one to aspire to lead. The difference manifests itself in the care taken by the servant first to make sure that others' highest priority needs are being served." The characteristics of a SL are based on carrying the needs of those they serve forward, giving their followers the ability to progress and develop.[342]

> Here again he hints that strife and party-spirit, love of rule and presumptuousness, had been the causes of their error, for the desire of rule is the mother of heresies. By saying, "Be servants one to another," he shows that the evil had arisen from this presumptuous and arrogant spirit, and therefore he applies a corresponding remedy. As your divisions arose from your desire to domineer over each other, "serve one another;" thus will ye be reconciled again. (Saint John Chrysostom[343])

Servant leadership, in the context of transformational leadership behaviors, encourages personal initiative and task performance.[344] Among the other powerful benefits of servant leadership on the follower is that it reduces instances of burnout,[345, 346] a serious psychological issue in the workplace characterized by emotional and physical fatigue,[347] by mitigating negative emotional interactions and reducing the external factors that lead to burnout that are in the leader's scope of control.[348]

---

[340] Rabindranath Tagore (1861–1941) was the Nobel Prize winner in literature in 1913.
[341] 1977.
[342] Spears 2005.
[343] Commentary on the Epistle to the Galatians 5:13.
[344] Judge and Piccolo 2004.
[345] Figure 16.
[346] Rude 2003.
[347] Shirom 2003.
[348] Maslach, Schaufeli, and Leiter 2001.

AUTHORITY IS DISTRIBUTABLE.

Servant leaders empower their followers. There is no valid reason not to allow your subordinates to make decisions and to follow through on those decisions. Empowerment will allow them to become wiser by learning from their mistakes and successes. Decentralizing the day-to-day operations of your work unit will allow for more agile operations while giving younger or less experienced individuals the opportunity to stretch their wings.

Servanthood is inextricably linked to the appreciation of human dignity. Equality of persons, regardless of their immutable characteristics,[349] is a given for those practicing the Living Your Leadership paradigm.

Father Peter Claver[350] served the African slaves coming to the new world. He would go to the ships as they docked at Cartagena, Colombia, and to the warehouses, bringing with him medicine, clothes, food, and water. He served in that capacity for twenty-seven years until his death. Servanthood does not only apply to our own handpicked followers. We are called to be servants to all, especially those in most need.

> We must speak to them with our hands,
> before we try to speak to them with our lips.
> —St. Peter Claver, SJ

> Stories about how a leader's self-sacrifice has had a profound positive effect on followers are common throughout history. Self-sacrificial leadership behaviors communicate an unambiguous message that the leader has an orientation that is pro-organization and, more to the point, follower-centric.[351] A servant leader *always* puts the needs of the followers before their own.

> Service before self is that virtue within us all which elevates the human spirit, compels us to reach beyond our meager selves to attach our spirit to something bigger than we are.
> —General John P. Jumper, 17th CSAF

Depending on the job being performed, servant leaders may well put

---

[349] Among these are race, color, national origin, religion, or sex.
[350] For more about his life and mission, visit http://catholicism.org/slave-of-slaves.html.
[351] De Cremer, van Knippenberg, van Dijke, and Bos 2006.

the mission above themselves as well. Servant leaders are not interested in promoting themselves. They do not care to preserve their power but to use their power (read: influence) to better the lives of their followers and accomplish the mission. It is likely that the surrender of power, counterintuitively, results in greater power in the person of the leader, as they are more likely to have gained influence through their self-sacrificial and altruistic actions.

The more one forgets himself
- by giving himself to a cause to serve or another person to love -
the more human he is and the more he actualizes himself.
—Viktor Frankl[352]

My time in Iraq was a humbling and eye-opening experience for me. My experiences in North America had in no way prepared me for the transition to the Middle East. The concrete barriers, oppressive dust that was so fine it turned into a paste when wet, and camel spiders the size of dinner plates were just some of the new and exciting experiences the country had to offer. Here is an excerpt from a letter to my wife describing the journey to my FOB:

> It gets dark early in the winter in the desert. This place has already left an indelible impression on me with its awkward concrete structures rimmed with barbed wire, the late afternoon sky set ablaze by the setting sun, and the dust. Dust is everywhere. I should explain more about the sky. It is beautiful, but would seem strange to you. Imagine driving down HWY 50 into Sacramento. In the heart of the city, it is smoggier than you have ever seen it, but the smog is not caused solely by emissions. Rather, the filth in the sky is comprised of the ever present dust and of the detritus of civilization. It forms an impenetrable, translucent layer that positively shimmers in the heat. (Tuesday, October 7, 2008)

I mentioned that a piece of my soul would go with the soldiers when they exited the FOB for convoy operations. Sometimes they didn't come back whole. My job was electronic warfare officer and instructor. This means that I was responsible for the vehicle jamming systems that were employed against

---

[352] 1963, p. 133.

radio-controlled improvised explosive devices (RCIEDs). I also trained soldiers on the proper operation and troubleshooting of those devices.

In the theater of operations, bravery seemed almost routine. These young men and women would put themselves in harm's way to shield their fellow service members. They traveled all over the city and beyond, protecting the local populace from terror threats. The stoicism of the company commanders remain a model for me to attempt to emulate, their calm exterior shielding their almost obsessive planning and care for their troops.

Just as those company commanders were authentically committed to their troops, willing to face any danger for them, your authenticity must be seamlessly woven throughout your leadership practice. You may never lead a team into combat, but you will stand in front of your team and lead with your words and actions. Make them real, make them count.

Leader self-sacrifice should not be tied to any specific context. You should never have to think to yourself, *Because I'm in this situation with these particular people, I would choose to act self-sacrificially.* That negates the authenticity of the act. Any person who sees that you are uninterested in treating all people with the same dignity will disbelieve your commitment to self-sacrifice. You must be willing to subordinate your ego, engage your humble self, and act as a servant to all.

In the same way that a leader makes a conscious decision to be a servant, the choice should be made to make sacrifices, though that is often not the case.[353]

A LEADER IS NOT MANIPULATIVE.

If a leader publicizes their self-sacrificial behavior, it is a sure bet that they do not authentically espouse the value of self-sacrifice. If they make a big deal out of their self-sacrificial behavior, then they are likely attempting to manipulatively earn a reciprocal response from their followers.[354] A leader does not worry about the WIIFM (What's in it for me?) question. A servant leader never encourages reciprocity for self-sacrificial behavior.[355]

---

[353] Matteson and Irving 2006.
[354] Choi and Mai-Dalton 1998.
[355] Matteson and Irving 2006.

CARING FOR FOLLOWERS SHOULD SUPERSEDE ANY TANGIBLE OR INTANGIBLE RECIPROCAL BENEFIT.

These two criteria are like the pillars of true love: deeds, and the gift of self.
—Pope Francis[356]

Taking meals after your employees has a long tradition, from biblical King David[357] to George Washington, but is this behavior in a time of plenty anything more than false humility? Its history is well-known, which makes the traditional act seem like an attempt to draw on the legitimacy of past great leaders. Self-sacrificial behaviors should be meaningful and linked to the needs of followers and to the setting, rather than an empty gesture. If there is plenty of food but not plenty of time (a more typical modern occurrence), which would more likely show your followers that you care about them, spending the plentiful commodity or the scarce one?

Leaders show up early, they work hard on their tasks, and they go home late. Burnout among high-performing leaders (and employees) is a real danger, even in an exciting and engaging work environment. Do not work late for the sake of working late. That is inefficient. Especially do not work late so that your followers can see you doing it. That is inauthentic behavior. Take the time required to do the job right.[358]

SELF-SACRIFICE SHOULD HURT A BIT.

When performed authentically, self-sacrificial behaviors engender trust and are powerful examples that followers will talk about. They will try their best to emulate those behaviors. As a side effect, those followers will begin to develop a mind-set that involves humility, a recognition of the equality of persons, and their place as servants.

When there are useful tasks back on the base, tasks that will allow your troops to grow and experience praise for a job well done, that is not the time to do work for them. Like a good parent, mastery experiences are encouraged in their children, while dangerous situations demand intervention. Delegation of authority, giving your followers opportunities to excel, is leading from behind.

---

[356] 6/7/13: Homily at the Mass of the Solemnity of the Most Sacred Heart of Jesus
[357] The Holy Bible 1984, 2 Samuel 23.
[358] Cockerell 2008.

That is demanded of any good mentor and leader, but it is not the whole equation.

When a company commander is the first through a door in a combat situation, their soldiers are more likely to *want* to follow their example. That leader is self-sacrificially taking the brunt of the initial danger. Especially in command and control situations, like the military, you can simply order someone to perform a task. Your example will always be far more impactful. Authentic and meaningful self-sacrifice is inspirational. [359]

It is better to lead from behind and to put others in front,
especially when you celebrate victory when nice things occur.
You take the front line when there is danger.
Then people will appreciate your leadership.
—Nelson Mandela

Altruism views leadership through the lens of benefit to the follower, whereas self-sacrifice pivots on the loss to the leader.[360] One of the critical links between others and self during the development of leadership attributes and skills is the image that you project. Not only should your image be authentic inasmuch as your actions reflect your true characteristics, but you must be constantly vigilant to maintain your integrity because whatever you project is what will be perceived by others. Practicing leader self-sacrifice by giving up power or privilege will be interpreted by your followers as an act of selflessness inspired by humility. It will serve to reduce the social distance between the leader and their followers.[361]

Miss no single opportunity of making some small sacrifice,
here by a smiling look, there by a kindly word; always
doing the smallest right and doing it all for love."
—Thérèse de Lisieux

PERCEPTION IS REALITY.

Self-sacrifice, or any other attribute, is only useful if they are evident to others. This sentence can be a painful revelation. You are worthwhile, your

[359] Choi and Mai-Dalton 1998, p. 475.
[360] Choi and Mai-Dalton 1998.
[361] Choi and Mai-Dalton 1998.

contributions make a difference, and the time you spend on self-improvement has value. As a leader, the utility of your actions is determined by the perception of others.

Oftentimes, our ego, informed by an inflated sense of self, can lead us to believe that because we feel that our actions match our intentions, others see what we are doing in the same way we see what we are doing. You know that you are proud of your people, but how do they know that you are proud of them? You have to show it through your words and actions.

Placing the greater need of the group above their own desires is the mark of a leader employing self-sacrificial behaviors.

> Leaders we admire do not place themselves at the center; they place others there. They do not seek the attention of people; they give it to others. They do not focus on satisfying their own aims and desires; they look for ways to respond to the needs and interests of their constituents. They are not self-centered, they concentrate on the constituent ... Leaders serve a purpose and the people who have made it possible for them to lead ... In serving a purpose, leaders strengthen credibility by demonstrating that they are not in it for themselves; instead, they have the interests of the institution, department or team and its constituents at heart. Being a servant may not be what many leaders had in mind where they choose to take responsibility for the vision and direction of their organization or team, but serving others is the most glorious and rewarding of all leadership tasks. (James Kouzes and Barry Posner[362])

It is an old adage that a leader accepts none of the credit and all of the blame. These sayings stick around; it is because they have a grain of truth to them. A high-performing team trusts its leadership. Build the faith in your team that things will be taken care of by their managers by following through. Use the word *we* to describe success and *I* to describe blame. That is not to say that your employees can do nothing wrong. Obviously, the progressive disciplinary process exists for a reason.

No man will make a great leader who wants to do it all himself,

---

[362] Kouzes and Posner 1993, p. 185.

or to get all the credit for doing it.

—Andrew Carnegie

When the leader can accept a blow to their ego by accepting blame when something does not go right, they act as a shield between their employees and the criticism of outsiders. It is a sign of immaturity when a person is unable to accept blame for something that happened because of their actions. Conversely, acting selflessly and sharing the credit for achievements will pay untold benefits in team esprit de corps and loyalty.[363] Though you recognize that you are not responsible for the thing you take blame for, ultimately, leaders are accountable.

Accountability implies acknowledgment of your role in a situation, good or bad. A solid sense of self, developed through self-reflection, means that you have the ability to take a step outside of your ego. By subordinating your ego, you can accept responsibility for something that may or may not have been directly attributable to you, as the leader. The subordination of ego applies here in the same manner that it does when you are humble.

A HUMBLE LEADER ACCEPTS BLAME AND DISTRIBUTES CREDIT.

You just took a new job and are excited about being able to exercise your brand of servant leadership with your staff. You have not met any of them yet, as they are in a different service area, but you are sure that your leadership values will translate. In the minds of those you will be leading, you feel like a less than likely candidate to lead their tribe. However, from the standpoint of leader self-sacrifice and effectiveness,[364] a less prototypical leader will benefit from higher productivity levels and effectiveness ratings.

As someone Living Your Leadership, you can walk into any leadership scenario and succeed. The foundation of the Living Your Leadership paradigm is Self-Leadership. Self-Leadership is a steady platform from which to exercise the flexibility that is inherent in the model. Your authentic self, the sum of your experiences, choices, self-knowledge, and self-determination make *your leadership* unique. A servant leader is not concerned with how uncomfortable a leadership scenario is. They are sure of themselves and their mission to serve first.

---

[363] Hayward 2007.
[364] Van Knippenberg and van Knippenberg 2005.

CHAPTER RECAP

Servant leadership begins and ends with caring.

- Servant leaders consciously build their followers into servant leaders in their turn.
- Move beyond the theoretical by practicing servant behaviors.
- The servant leader is humble and willing to listen. They lead through influence and cooperation.
- Self-sacrificial behaviors are normal for servant leaders.
- Servant leaders do not manipulate their followers. Ethics define the center of the practice.
- Accountability means taking blame. A servant leader empowers their followers, freely giving credit while accepting more than their fair share of any blame.

The challenge of leadership is to be strong, but not rude;
be kind, but not weak;
be bold, but not bully;
be thoughtful, but not lazy;
be humble, but not timid;
be proud, but not arrogant;
have humor, but without folly.
—Jim Rohn

DENOUEMENT

PITFALLS

Before it is an honor, leadership is trust;
Before it is a call to glory,
Leadership is a call to service;
... before all else, forever and always,
leadership is a willingness to serve.
—Father Edson Wood, OSA, cadet Catholic chaplain[365]

You cannot offer the best of your authentic self without exposing your failures and vulnerabilities. This is the reason that *leading yourself* is the first half of the book. A leader has to develop themselves, to internally reconcile their failings, and to own their narrative before authenticity can be achieved. The power of vulnerability and the important role of shame are described nowhere better than by Brené Brown.[366] She is a qualitative researcher who has, for more than a decade, studied the effects of shame in our culture and our individual lives.

EGOTISM

A self-assured leader is either (1) false or (2) someone who has accepted their past and grown from it. The odds in favor of the latter are not great. Self-assurance should buoy a leader, putting a damper on self-doubt. In many cases,

---

[365] Invocation at Assumption of Command, US Military Academy, August 11, 2004.
[366] Brown 2012.

self-assured leaders are simply cocky. They lead without having done the hard self-development work. When someone is leading without having bothered to develop themselves, their ego will guarantee wildly unpredictable and probably unhealthy leadership behaviors.

> Being open with your insecurities paradoxically makes you more confident and charismatic around others. The pain of honest confrontation is what generates the greatest trust and respect in your relationships. Suffering through your fears and anxieties is what allows you to build courage and perseverance. (Mark Manson[367])

FEAR

It would be foolish to say that successful leaders do not experience fear. Everyone experiences fear in one way or another. A successful leader will take that experience of fear, analyze and determine its antecedents, and use that negative emotion in a positive way. Fear should be transmuted into inspirational courage.

NARCISSISM

Transformational leadership has a serious risk of narcissism and undue influence. The use of idealized influence by a charismatic individual is potent. As the charismatic leader, your strength of personality impacts the level of influence you have on followers. Using your personality to influence others isn't inherently bad. There are several reasons to avoid leading solely by personality, however.

If the strength of your personality is all that people choose to follow, they will be bereft if you leave the organization. If you do not have a tight grip on your ego, using appropriate self-regulatory behaviors, you may start to believe that you are owed something (loyalty, respect, submission) based on your own merit. That narcissism can lead to manipulative behaviors and corruption, especially if it is coupled with a lack of reflection.[368] Transformational leadership is not

---

[367] Manson 2016.
[368] Giampetro et al. 1998.

alone in the pitfall arena. Servant leadership and self-leadership, despite their power, flexibility, and depth, are also subject to failings in execution.

RECIPROCITY

Servant leadership can also be fraught with unanticipated consequences and dangers. One of these dangers is the idea of servant-leader reciprocity. A servant leader serves their followers. Due to rendering that service, there is an inherent psychological obligation to the leader from the follower.[369] From the individual served to the leader who has served them, there exists the feeling of a debt that should be paid. This feeling of obligation is transactional in nature and is probably an explanation for why transactional leadership *feels* natural to many people. The problem with that reciprocal relationship is that a servant leader's job is not to create indebtedness in their followers but to encourage their followers to become servants themselves.

LIES

Dishonesty seems like something that should be simple to avoid. In practice, it is all too common. Little white lies and omissions corrupt an organization's transparency. They damage the trust and loyalty that followers have in a leader. Building and encouraging an atmosphere of open and honest feedback will make backstabbing and political, passive-aggressive behavior much more rare.[370] When candor is employed, there are few secrets to leverage for political gain. Few lies survive courageous conversations.

DISRESPECT

Disrespect is commonly used by the insecure and the weak. As a leader, you should never tolerate disrespect amongst your followers or to you. Showing a lack of respect for another person in your organization is enormously damaging to the morale of the unit. Disrespect comes in many forms. Some of the more common instances to look out for are gossip, condescension, or the formation of exclusive cliques. In an organization where respect is practiced, an atmosphere

---

[369] Cialdini 2001.
[370] Scott 2017.

of mutual cooperation and trust will endure. Disrespect eats away at the esprit de corps of an organization.

INGRATITUDE

Ingratitude is one of the cardinal sins of leadership. Any self-aware leader should understand that they did not get to where they are solely by chance or their own hard work. Humble leaders understand that they have been propped up by those they have led and by the mentors, friends, and professional connections that they have made along the way. A leader who displays ingratitude often focuses on themselves. *Their* contributions are paramount. That leader will not reward their followers for their effort if it undermines the leader's perceived self-worth. Ingratitude leads directly to narcissism and egotism.

FAVORITISM

If you want to destroy trust in your leadership, employ favoritism. Favoritism takes many shapes, including cronyism and nepotism. If you have a team of ten individuals, do not spend 90 percent of your time with three or four of them. Do not take one or two of them to lunch and ignore the rest on a routine basis. Spend time talking with each of them.

Make sure that the time that you do spend, especially with those who you may not like as much, is visible to the entire team. You have to be genuine in your care and concern for those individuals. If you are not able to be genuine, then you will have to do some self-reflection concerning the inherent value of human dignity.

Any leader who thinks that their team does not see the amount of time that they spend with one or another of their peers is delusional. Your followers know the amount of time, effort, and care that you bestow on each of them. They are much more likely to give you the benefit of the doubt if you have taken steps to ensure that you are not showing favoritism.

POOR COMMUNICATION

You have likely heard it before: communication is key. Communication allows you to keep everyone informed about your vision, goals, objectives, and plans of action. Confusion about roles and responsibilities or tasks and expectations are most often due to a lack of communication.

Something to consider: a lack of communication may not be as detrimental to your leadership as poor communication. Being professional and forthright in communication to your followers and to your superiors is absolutely necessary. Confusion can be avoided, and clarity can be achieved as long as you are brief yet complete in the way that you email, speak, write, and otherwise communicate.

BREVITY BREEDS CLARITY.

With regard to email and other forms of remote communication, they are not as effective or meaningful as meeting face-to-face interactions.

> You will never get the whole picture from a
> report, e-mail, or phone conversation.
> Looking at men and women in the eye will give you a good
> sense of your team and how they are performing.
> —Command Sergeant Major Donald J. Freeman, United States Army

Just because you send an email does *not* mean that you have effectively led. Mechanical sending and receiving of messages is not communication.[371] Email is a useful tool, but it is not the end-all and be-all of workplace communication.

The overuse of email can make a leader seem disingenuous and detached. Email communication is useful up to a point, but we all have seen inboxes get crowded with dozens or hundreds of emails every day, which can definitely lead to a marked decrease in productivity.[372]

A majority of human communication occurs in the form of nonverbal cues and body language. When you interact solely via email, the communication contains less information for a recipient to make a clear decision about. If you are not a very careful wordsmith, you will inadvertently cause misunderstanding. Now, instead of having easily communicated something, you have created workplace conflict, which detracts from the level of trust and cooperation in your environment.

---

[371] De Pree 1989.
[372] LugoSantiago 2014.

RIGIDITY

Earlier in the book, you read about flexibility as a trait to be sharpened and exercised by leaders. The flipside of flexibility is rigidity. You should not be flexible with regard to your vision and your ethical values. However, you must be flexible and adaptable in your methods. Followers who notice that leaders are rigid and inflexible often feel, for good reason, that their leaders are no better than faceless managers.

That is to say that a machine could very likely do the *leader's* work. If you are practicing management by exception[373] or leading from a spreadsheet, then you are rigid. Flexible leaders know the value of foresight and use various innovative methods to get the job done.

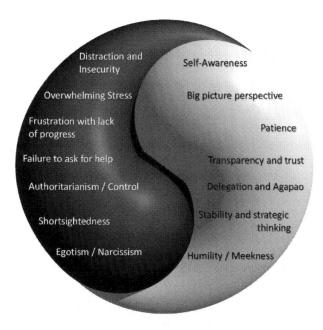

Figure 17. Balance in Living Your Leadership

---

[373] Transactional management practice. Deviations from planned results or expected behavior are escalated to management and dealt with on a case-by-case basis.

WRAP-UP: LIVING YOUR LEADERSHIP

The True Gentleman is the man whose conduct proceeds from good
will and an acute sense of propriety and whose self-control is equal
to all emergencies; who does not make the poor man conscious of his
poverty, the obscure man of his obscurity, or any man of his inferiority or
deformity; who is himself humbled if necessity compels him to humble
another; who does not flatter wealth, cringe before power, or boast of his
own possessions or achievements; who speaks with frankness but always
with sincerity and sympathy; whose deed follows his word; who thinks
of the rights and feelings of others rather than his own; and who appears
well in any company; a man with whom honor is sacred and virtue safe.
—John Walter Wayland, 1899

Concurrent with my military and civilian service, I achieved the rank of associate professor and have taught and developed undergraduate and graduate curriculum at multiple universities. I've had the opportunity to observe thousands of students as they proceed through their academic journeys. I was privileged to stand up and am now the director of the master's in human resource management program at a university. As an academician, entrepreneur, corporate leader, and combat veteran, the Living Your Leadership model for management consulting is firmly cemented in my own practice.

My unique experience as an officer, manager, director, professor, and consultant has demonstrated to me that we all start in different places. A single, unifying theory for personal growth and leadership has to start with what we all have in common—ourselves. Moving from the development of self, it is natural and logical to proceed with a more general approach to leadership practice, one that is holistic and practicable but also general enough to apply to a variety of individuals.

These generalizations provide for the opportunity to incorporate tools that are applicable regardless of your current level of self-improvement or understanding of specific principles of leadership. Experience is the best teacher, but just making it through things does not guarantee you will be able to fully connect theory to practice. An experienced leader can still be a terrible leader. That is why reading and studying leadership texts from the world's past and present leadership experts and historians is so crucial, so that you can continue to learn and grow in your knowledge.

> Leadership and learning are indispensable to each other.
> —John F. Kennedy

Self-knowledge, perfecting the precepts and practices of self-leadership, enables personal growth. That foundational understanding and critical reflection will allow for the practice of transformational and servant leadership. A word of caution: just reading a book like this one does not mean that you will improve. As Lao-tzu wrote, "A Sage will practice the Tao. A fool will only admire it."[374]

> One's philosophy is not best expressed in words;
> it is expressed in the choices one makes.
> In the long run, we shape our lives and we shape ourselves.
> The process never ends until we die.
> And the choices we make are ultimately our own responsibility.
> —Eleanor Roosevelt

As business continues to move upward and onward, expanding global interconnectedness, the leadership in every organization should be equipped and ready to handle day-to-day challenges. Diversity of the global workforce means that a more inclusive understanding of leadership is needed. Leadership has changed greatly over the last few decades. The charismatic, dictatorial leader is no longer viewed as the best choice for global organizations of tomorrow.

---

[374] 1996.

Leadership is trending toward the transformational and servant styles. The need to have someone with integrity, empathy, self-awareness, and the understanding of others moves organizations in a direction that keeps employees motivated and committed. Motivating employees to achieve organizational goals through delegation and empowerment aids in employee satisfaction and retention. Maintaining employees on the workforce saves the cost of training, lawsuits, recruitment efforts, and extrinsic incentives.

LEADERSHIP CAN BE LEARNED AND IMPROVED UPON.

Mastery of the skills outlined in this text enhance the ability to lead. Leading with humility and openness will engender loyalty and trust in leadership. Without dedicated followers, leaders will not be able to accomplish up to expectations. Leadership is alchemy. When organizational chaos or oppressive hierarchy comes into contact with servanthood, a change in the substance of the organization occurs. It presages a positive change in culture.

A transformational leader exerts influence by broadening and elevating followers' goals and providing them with confidence to perform beyond the expectations specified in the implicit or explicit agreement.[375] The transformational leader exhibits charismatic behaviors, arouses inspirational motivation, provides intellectual stimulation, and treats followers with individualized consideration. Transformational leaders are also able to imbue work with meaning while communicating an inspirational vision for the organization.[376] The transformational leader has the ability to help followers reach their full potential, generating the highest levels of performance.[377]

> Project authenticity and vulnerability, be present, be accepting,
> and see your role as being useful, as being the servant.
> —James A. Autry[378]

The servant leader is defined by Greenleaf as *first* being a servant. The characteristics that are attributed to a servant leader and central to their development are listening, empathy, healing, awareness, persuasion, conceptualization, foresight, stewardship, commitment to growth of people,

---

[375] Bass and Avolio 1994.
[376] Bass 1985.
[377] Dvir, Eden, Avolio, and Shamir 2002.
[378] From *Practicing Servant Leadership*.

and building community.[379] The practice of Living Your Leadership hinges on the conscious choices that you choose to make each day.

> Man constantly makes his choice concerning the mass of present potentialities; which of these will be condemned to nonbeing and which will be actualized? Which choice will be made an actuality once and forever, an immortal "footprint in the sands of time"? At any moment, man must decide, for better or for worse, what will be the monument of his existence. (Viktor Frankl[380])

Both transformational and servant styles focus on followers and how leaders can help them to develop and reach their full potentials. Each share similar attributes, but transformational leadership tends to place a greater emphasis on organizational goals. The servant leader is more often associated with public service industries, while the transformational leader is seen more often in business settings.

> The content of most textbooks is perishable,
> but the tools of self-directedness serve one well over time.
> —Albert Bandura

Living Your Leadership journey does not end when you put down this volume. My hope is that you incorporate the practices you have read in these pages into your daily practice, that you explore the suggested readings, and that you seek to serve in all you do.

Thank you!
Chris Ewing

> The first responsibility of a leader is to define reality.
> The last is to say thank you.
> In between, the leader is a servant.
> —Max De Pree

---

[379] Greenleaf 2002.
[380] 1963, p. 143.

ACKNOWLEDGMENTS

Like any human endeavor, this book didn't simply spring from the mind and fingertips of the author. It has been an iterative process, and I would be remiss not to acknowledge some of the main contributors to the project.

Dr. Jamiel Vadell, whose enthusiasm and optimism fueled this journey. Jamiel has been my friend and mentor since the day he took me on my first nuclear alerts to the Alternate Command Post while we were stationed together in Minot AFB, North Dakota. Jamiel has been my boss and has seen me at my best and at my worst. He is my brother in the truest sense of the word.

Major Christopher "Braden" Stutheit, USAF, and Major Linn VanWoerkom, USAFR, for their consultation and contribution to this work related to nuclear operations. These gentlemen legitimately care about their roles as leaders.

Lieutenant Colonel Charley "Chuck" Morris, who started me thinking about leadership in in ROTC all those years ago. Having had no tangible example in my personal life, Chuck was first *leader* I worked with. His continued success as a pilot and commander in the USAF is testament to his adherence to the principles he taught us cadets so many years ago.

Michelle Reinstatler, English language and literature savant. Because of Michelle, I wasn't the only cadet to have chosen an English major in AFROTC.

Colonel Marné Deranger, USAF (retired), for her mentorship and support. I've already talked about her contributions to my theories and experience in the text, so I won't belabor it here.

Robert J. Gore, executive leader and editor par excellence. This book would not have assumed its final state without the invaluable guidance he provided from his distinguished career.

Colonel Jed Davis, USAF (retired), for his leadership during difficult times. I learned more from your example than you will ever know.

Thank you seems inadequate for my wife, Missy. She has spent years listening to my ideas and my complaints, editing my work, and talking over the idea of becoming an author.

ABBREVIATIONS

AFB—Air Force Base
AFM—Air Force Manual
AOM—Academy of Management
AOR—area of responsibility
APA—American Psychological Association
ASV—American Standard Version
DV—distinguished visitors
EQ—emotional intelligence
FOB—forward operating base
FRLD—full range leadership development
ICBM—intercontinental ballistic missile
ICE—integrity, courage, empathy
KJV—King James Version
LCC—launch control center
LMS—learning management system
MBE—management by exception
MBWA—management by walking around
MLQ—multifactor leadership questionnaire
NIV—New International Version
QLRC—Quality of Life Research Center
RCA—root cause analysis
RCIED—radio-controlled improvised explosive devices
ROTC—Reserve Officer Training Corps
SJ—Society of Jesus
SL—servant leadership
SLI—Servant Leader Institute
SMART—specific, measurable, actionable, and time-bound
SME—subject matter expert

TWA—Trans World Airlines
WSSR—weapon system safety rules
USAF—United States Air Force
ZPD—zone of proximal development

REFERENCES

Air Force Instruction (AFI) 91-114. 2015. "Safety Rules for the Intercontinental Ballistic Missile System." June 30. www.e-publishing.af.mil.

Albion, M. S. 2006. *True to Yourself: Leading a Values-Based Business.* San Francisco, CA: Berrett-Koehler.

Algera, P. M., and M. Lips-Wiersma. 2012. "Radical authentic leadership: Cocreating the conditions under which all members of the organization can be authentic." *Leadership Quarterly* 23: 118–131.

Amar, A. 2009. "To Be a Better Leader, Give Up Authority." *Harvard Business Review* 87, no. 12: 22–24.

August, V. 2001. *Know Thyself, Show Thyself: A Guide to Becoming the Person You've Always Dreamed of Being.* San Jose: Writers Club Press.

Baltes, P .B., and H. W. Reese. 1984. "The Life-Span Perspective in Developmental Psychology." In *Developmental Psychology: An Advanced Textbook,* edited by M. H. Bornstein and M. E. Lamb, 493–531. Hillsdale, NJ: Erlbaum.

Bandura, A. 1978. "The self-system in reciprocal determinism." *American Psychologist* 33: 344–358.

Bandura, A. 1986. *Social Foundations of Thought and Action: A Social Cognitive Theory.* Englewood Cliffs, NJ: Prentice Hall.

Bandura, A. 1989. "Social Cognitive Theory." In Vol. 6 of *Annals of Child Development:*

Six Theories of Child Development, edited by R. Vasta, 1–60. Greenwich, CT: JAI Press.

Bartlett, F. 1932. *Remembering.* Cambridge: Cambridge University Press.

Bass, B. M. 1998. *Transformational Leadership; Industry, Military, and Educational Impact.* Lawrence Erlbaum Associates, Mahwah, NJ.

Bass, B. M., and P. Steidlmeier. 1999. "Ethics, Character, and Authentic Transformational

Leadership Behavior." *Leadership Quarterly* 10, no. 2: 181–217.

Beatty, B. R., and C. R. Brew. 2004. "Trusting relationships and emotional epistemologies: a foundational leadership issue." *School Leadership and Management* 24, no. 3: 329–356. doi:10.1080/136324304200 0266954.

Bell, G. B., and H. E. Hall Jr. 1954. "The relationship between leadership and empathy." *Journal of Abnormal and Social Psychology* 49, no. 1: 156–157. doi:10.1037/h0053927.

Bennis, W. G. 2007. "The challenge of leadership in the modern world." *American Psychologist Association* 62, no. 1: 2–5.

Bennis, W. G., and R. J. Thomas. 2002a. "Crucibles of leadership." *Harvard Business Review* 80, no. 9: 39–45.

Bennis, W. G., and R. J. Thomas. 2002b. "Leadership crucibles." *Executive Excellence* 19, no. 11: 3–4.

Berkovich, I. 2014. "Between person and person: Dialogical pedagogy in authentic leadership development." *Academy of Management Learning and Education* 13, no. 2: 245–264.

Brown, M. E., and L. K. Treviño. 2006. "Ethical leadership: A review and future directions." *Leadership Quarterly* 17: 595–616.

Brown, R. 2012. "The Power of Vulnerability: Teachings on Authenticity, Connection, and Courage." [Audio Download]. Sounds True.

Burton, K. D., J. E. Lydon, D. U. D'Alessandro, and R. Koestner. 2006. "The differential effects of intrinsic and identified motivation on well-being and performance: Prospective, experimental, and implicit approaches to self-determination theory." *Journal of Personality and Social Psychology* 91, no. 4: 750–762.

Cameron, J., D. W. Pierce, K. M. Banko, and A. Gear. 2005. "Achievement-based rewards and intrinsic motivation: A test of cognitive mediators." *Journal of Educational Psychology* 97, no. 4: 641–655.

Campbell, D., and K. Campbell. 2011. "Impact of decision-making empowerment on attributions of leadership." *Military Psychology* 23, no. 2: 154–179. doi:10.1080/08995605.2011.550231.

Catholic Church. 1963. Peace on Earth: Encyclical letter of Pope John XXIII, "Pacem in Terris," 1963. London: Catholic Truth Society.

Catholic Church. 1995. *Catechism of the Catholic Church*. New York: Doubleday.

Caza, A., and B. Jackson. 2011. "Authentic Leadership." In *Sage Handbook of Leadership*, edited by D. Bryman, K. Collinson, B. Grint, B. Jackson B, and M. Uhl-Bien, 350–362. Thousand Oaks, CA: Sage.

Center for Creative Leadership. 2008. "The Role of Power in Effective Leadership." [White Paper]. http://www.ccl.org/leadership/pdf/research/roleOfPower.pdf.

Center for Creative Leadership. 2012. "The Care and Feeding of the Leader's Brain." [White Paper]. http://www.ccl.org/leadership/pdf/research/CareFeedingLeadersBrain.pdf.

Chan, D. W. 2007. "Leadership and Intelligence." *Roeper Review* 29, no. 3: 183–189.

Chandler, C. L., and J. P. Connell. 1987. "Children's intrinsic, extrinsic and internalized motivation: A developmental study of children's reasons for liked and disliked behaviours." *British Journal of Developmental Psychology* 5: 357–365.

Chemers, M. M., C. B. Watson, and S. T. May. 2000. "Dispositional affect and leadership effectiveness: A comparison of self-esteem, optimism, and efficacy." *Personality and Social Psychology Bulletin* 26: 267–277.

Chen, W., and R. Jacobs. 1997. *Competence Study*. Boston, MA: Hay/McBer.

Cialdini, R. B. 2001. *Influence: Science and Practice*. Needham Heights, MA: Allyn and Bacon.

Choi, Y., and R. R. Mai-Dalton. 1998. "On the leadership function of self-sacrifice." *Leadership Quarterly* 9, no. 4: 475–501.

Cockerell, L. 2008. *Creating Magic: 10 Common Sense Leadership Strategies from a Life at Disney*. New York: Currency Doubleday.

Collins, J. 2001b. "Level 5 leadership: The triumph of humility and fierce resolve." *Harvard Business Review* 79: no. 1: 67–76.

Cordova, D. I., and M. Lepper. 1996. "Intrinsic motivation and the process of learning: Beneficial effects of contextualization, personalization, and choice." *Journal of Educational Psychology* 88, no. 4: 715–730.

Crant, J. M., and T. S. Bateman. 2000. "Charismatic leadership viewed from above: the impact of proactive personality." *Journal of Organizational Behavior* 21: 63–75.

Crom, M. 1998. "The leader as servant." *Training* 35, no. 7 (July): 6–10.

Csikszentmihalyi, M. 1990. *Flow: The Psychology of Optimal Experience*. New York: Harper and Row.

Deal, J. J., S. Stawiski, W. Gentry, and K. L. Cullen. 2013. "What makes a leader effective?" Center for Creative Leadership. October. http://www.ccl.org/leadership/pdf/research.pdf.

Dempsey, M. E. 2017. "Leadership Instincts: Listen, Amplify, Include." [LinkedIn Pulse article]. August 25. https://www.linkedin.com/

pulse/leadership-instincts-listen-amplify-include-general-martin-e-dempsey.

Descartes, R. 1979. *Meditations on First Philosophy*. Translated by D. A. Cress. Indianapolis, IN: Hackett Publishing. (Originally published in 1641.)

Deci, E. L. 1971. "Effects of externally mediated rewards on intrinsic motivation." *Journal of Personality and Social Psychology* 18, no. 1: 105–115.

Deci, E. L., J. P. Connell, and R. M. Ryan. 1989. "Self-determination in a work organization." *Journal of Applied Psychology* 74: 580–590.

Deci, E. L., and R. M. Ryan. 1985. "The general causality orientations scale: Self-determination in personality." *Journal of Research in Personality* 19: 109–134.

De Charms, R. 1968. *Personal Causation: The Internal Affective Determinants of Behavior.* New York: Academic Press.

De Cremer, D., D. van Knippenberg, M. van Dijke, and A. E. R. Bos. 2006. "Self-sacrificial leadership and follower self-esteem: When collective identification matters." *Group Dynamics: Theory, Research, and Practice* 10, no. 3: 233–245.

Den Hartog, D., and F. Belschak. 2012. "When does transformational leadership enhance employee proactive behavior? The role of autonomy and role breadth self-efficacy." *Journal of Applied Psychology* 97, no. 1: 194–202.

Donohue, K. S., and L. Wong. 1994. "Understanding and Applying Transformational Leadership." *Military Review* 74, no. 8.

Dvir, T., D. Eden, B. J. Avolio, and B. Shamir. 2002. "Impact of transformational leadership on follower development and performance: A field experiment." *Academy of Management Journal* 45: 735–744.

Efron, L. May 11, 2015. "The Three Fundamental Leadership Traits That Support Enduring Organizations." https://www.forbes.com/sites/louisefron/2015/05/11/the-three-fundamental-leadership-traits-that-support-enduring-organizations/#46ad59fc4b7c.

Ewing, C. 2011. "Does causality orientation moderate the relationship between assignment choice and academic achievement in Air Force officers performing the nuclear mission?" Boca Raton, FL: Dissertation.com.

Farling, M. L., A. G. Stone, and B. E. Winston. 1999. "Servant leadership: Setting the stage for empirical research." *Journal of Leadership Studies*, 6, no. 1-2: 49–72.

Ferris, G. R., et al. 2005. "Development and validation of the political skill inventory." *Journal of Management* 31: 126–152.

Firth-Cozens, J., and D. Mowbray. 2001. "Leadership and the quality of care." *Quality in Health Care* 10: 3–7.

Gardner, W. L., B. J. Avolio, and F. O. Walumbwa. 2005. "Authentic leadership development: Emergent themes and future directions." In *Authentic Leadership Theory and Practice: Origins, Effects and Development*, edited by W. L. Gardner, B. J. Avolio, and F. O. Walumbwa, 387–406. London: Elsevier.

Gardner, W. L., and C. L. Cole. 1988. "Self-Monitoring Procedures." In *Behavioral Assessment in Schools*, edited by E. S. Shapiro and E. R. Kratochwoll, 206–246. New York: Guilford Press.

Giampetro, M. A., T. Brown, M. N. Browne, and N. Kubasek. 1998. "Do We Really Need More Leaders in Business?" *Journal of Business Ethics* 17, no. 15: 1727–1736.

Gill, M. 2008. *How Starbucks Saved My Life: A Son of Privilege Learns to Live Like Everyone Else*. London: Gotham Books.

Givens, R. J. 2008. "Transformational leadership: The impact on organizational and personal outcomes." *Emerging Leadership Journeys* 1, no. 1: 4–24.

Goldfein, D. L., and Air University (US). 1999. *Sharing Success—Owning Failure: Preparing to Command in the Twenty-First Century Air Force*. Maxwell Air Force Base, AL: Air University Press.

Goleman, D. 2004. "What Makes a Leader?" *Harvard Business Review* 82, no. 1: 82–91.

Gottlieb, J. Z., and J. Sanzgiri. 1996. "Towards an Ethical Dimension of Decision Making in Organizations." *Journal of Business Ethics* 15, no. 12: 1275–1285.

Graen, G. B., and M. Uhl-Bien. 1995. 'Relationship-based approach to leadership: Development of leader–member exchange (LMX) theory of leadership over 25 years: Applying a multilevel multidomain perspective." *Leadership Quarterly* 6: 219–247.

Graham, W. 1991. "Servant-leadership in organizations: Inspirational and moral." *Leadership Quarterly* 2, no. 2: 105–119.

Hayward, M. 2007. *Ego Check: Why Executive Hubris Is Wrecking Companies and Careers and How to Avoid the Trap*. Chicago: Kaplan Pub.

Headquarters, Department of the Army. 2006. *Army Leadership (FM 6-22)*. Washington, DC: Government Printing Office.

Herodotus. 2007. *The Landmark Herodotus: The Histories*. New York: Pantheon Books.

Howatson-Jones, I. 2004. "The servant leader." *Nursing Management (Harrow, London, England: 1994)* 11, no. 3: 20–24.

Howell, J. M., and B. J. Avolio. 1993. "Transformational leadership, transactional leadership, locus of control, and support for innovation: Key predictors of consolidated-business-unit performance." *Journal of Applied Psychology* 78, no. 6: 891–902. doi:10.1037/0021-9010.78.6.891.

Huber, R. 2007. *What Makes a Leader.* United States: America Star Books.

Hume, D. 2000. "Inquiry Concerning Human Understanding." In *Readings in Modern Philosophy Vol. II: Locke, Berkeley, Hume, and Associated Texts,* edited by Roger Ariew and Eric Watkins, 328–394. Indianapolis, IN: Hackett Publishing Company.

Irving, J. A. 2005. "Servant Leadership and the Effectiveness of Teams." Published dissertation, Regent University, School of Leadership Studies.

Johnson, R. D. 2003. "USAWC Strategy Research Project: Leadership." Carlisle Barracks, PA: US Army War College.

Judge, T. A., and R. F. Piccolo. 2004. "Transformational and transactional leadership: A meta-analytic test of their relative validity." *Journal of Applied Psychology* 89: 755–768.

Katzenbach, J. R. 1997. *Teams at the Top: Unleashing the Potential of Both Teams and Individual Leaders.* Boston: Harvard Business School Press.

Kellett, J. B., R. H. Humphrey, and R. G. Sleeth. 2006. "Empathy and the emergence of task and relations leaders." *Leadership Quarterly* 17, no. 2: 146–162.

Kernis, M., and B. Goldman. 2006. "A multicomponent conceptualization of authenticity: Theory and research." *Advances in Experimental Social Psychology* 38: 283–357.

Kiel, L., and D. J. Watson. 2009. "Affective Leadership and Emotional Labor: A View from the Local Level." *Public Administration Review* 69, no. 1: 22. doi:10.1111/j.1540-6210.2008.01936.x.

Kouzes, J. M., and B. Z. Posner. 1989. "Leadership Is in the Eye of the Follower." In *Developing Human Resources,* edited by J. William Pfeiffer. San Diego, California: University Associates.

Kriger, M., and Y. Seng. 2005. "Leadership with inner meaning: A contingency theory of leadership based on the worldviews of five religions." *Leadership Quarterly* 16: 771–806.

Kruse, K. 2013. "What is authentic leadership?" Forbes.com LLC. May 12. http://www.forbes.com/sites/kevinkruse/2013/05/12/what-is-authentic-leadership/.

Lad, L. J., and D. Luechauer. 1998. "On the Path to Servant-Leadership." In L. Spears, *Insights on Leadership: Service, Spirit, and Servant Leadership*. New York, NY: John Wiley.

Lee, H. 1960. *To Kill a Mockingbird*. Philadelphia: Lippincott.

Leonard, N. H., L. L. Beauvais, and R. W. Scholl. 1995. "A self-concept based model of work motivation." *Academy of Management Best Papers Proceedings*: 322–326. doi:10.5465/AMBPP.1995.17536607.

Lindebaum, D., and S. Cartwright. 2011. "Leadership effectiveness: The costs and benefits of being emotionally intelligent." *Leadership and Organizational Development Journal* 32, no. 3: 281–290.

Lorenz, S. R. 2012. *Lorenz on Leadership: Lessons on Effectively Leading People, Teams, and Organizations*. Maxwell AFB, United States: Air University Press, Air Force Research Institute.

LugoSantiago, J. A. 2014. *On the Leadership Journey: 30 Conversations about Leading Yourself and Others*. Maxwell AFB, United States: Air University, Air Force Research Institute.

Machiavelli, N., and H. C. Mansfield. 1998. *The Prince*. Chicago, IL: University of Chicago Press.

Maister, D. H. 2014. *Practice What You Preach: What Managers Must Do to Create a High Achievement Culture*. New York: Free Press.

Martinez, M. E. 2006. "What is metacognition?" *Phi Delta Kappan* 87, no. 9: 696–699.

Maslach, M., W. B. Schaufeli, and M. P. Leiter. 2001. "Job Burnout." *Annual Review Psychology* 52: 397–422.

Maslow, A. H. 1943. "A theory of human motivation." *Psychological Review* 50: 370–396.

Matteson, J., and J. Irving. 2006. "Servant versus self-sacrificial leadership: A behavioral comparison of two follower-oriented leadership theories." *International Journal of Leadership Studies* 2, no. 1: 36–51.

Mehrabian, A., and N. Epstein. 1972. "A measure of emotional empathy." *Journal of Personality* 40: 525–543.

Merton, T. 1972. *New Seeds of Contemplation*. New York, NY: New Directions.

Miyamoto, M., and V. Harris. 1974. *A Book of Five Rings*. New York: Overlook Press.

Montgomery III, W. H. 2007. "Beyond Words: Leader Self-awareness and Interpersonal Skills, USAWC Strategy Research Project." Carlisle Barracks, PA: Defense Technical Information Center, Army War College.

Nixon, M. M. 2005. "The servant leadership: Followership continuum from a social psychology cognitive perspective." *Proceedings of the Servant Leadership Research Roundtable*. http://www.regent.edu/acad/global/publications/sl_proceedings/.

Noddings, N. 1998. "Care and Moral Education." In *Critical Social Issues in American Education: Transformation in a Postmodern World*, edited by H. S. Shapiro and D. E. Purpel, 309–320. Mahwah, NJ: Lawrence Erlbaum Associates.

Page, D., and T. P. Wong. 2000. "A Conceptual Framework for Measuring Servant Leadership." In *The Human Factor in Shaping the Course of History and Development*, edited by S. Abjibolosoo. Lanham, MD: University Press of America.

Parry, K. W., and S. B. Proctor-Thomson. 2002. "Perceived integrity of transformational leaders in organisational settings." *Journal of Business Ethics* 35, no. 2: 75–96.

Patterson, K. A. 2003. "Servant leadership: a theoretical model." *Servant Leadership Roundtable*. Virginia Beach: Regent University.

Peters, T. J., and R. H. Waterman. 1982. *In Search of Excellence: Lessons from America's Best-Run Companies*. New York, NY: Harper and Row.

Peterson, C., and M. E. P. Seligman. 2004. *Character Strengths and Virtues: A Handbook and Classification*. New York: Oxford University Press and Washington, DC: American Psychological Association. www.viacharacter.org.

Pfeffer, J., and R. I. Sutton. 2000. *The Knowing-Doing Gap: How Smart Companies Turn Knowledge into Action*. Boston, MA: Harvard Business School Press.

Poon, R. 2006. "A model for servant leadership, self-efficacy and mentorship." In *Proceedings of the 2006 Servant Leadership Research Roundtable*.

Poore, J. October 2012. "The STAR Leader's Role in Creating Exceptional Experiences." Speech presented at Kaiser Permanente STAR Leader Forum, San Jose, CA.

Posner, M. I., and S. J. Boies. 1971. "Components of attention." *Psychological Review* 78, no. 5: 391–408. http://dx.doi.org/10.1037/h0031333.

Ringma, C., and I. Alexander. 2015. *Of Martyrs, Monks, and Mystics: A Yearly Meditational Reader of Ancient Spiritual Wisdom*. Eugene, OR: Wipf and Stock Publishers.

Rockwell, D. 2012. [Web log message]. November 8. http://leadershipfreak.wordpress.com/2012/11/08/facing-the-3-pressing-challenges-of-leadership/.

Rockwell, D. 2013. [Web log message]. February 1. http://leadershipfreak. wordpress.com/2013/02/01/how-to-motivate-the-unmotivated/.

Rosenberg, M. 1979. *Conceiving the Self.* New York: Basic Books.

Rosenberg, M. B. 2015. *Nonviolent Communication: A Language of Life.* Encinitas, CA: PuddleDancer Press.

Rotter, J. B. 1966. "Generalized expectancies for internal versus external locus of control of reinforcement." In *Psychological Monographs: General and Applied,* SO (Whole No. 609).

Rude, W. 2003. "Paradoxical leadership: The impact of servant-leadership on burnout of staff." *Proceedings of the Servant Leadership Research Roundtable.* http://www.regent.edu/acad/global/publications/ sl_proceedings/.

Ryan, R. M. 1995. "Psychological needs and the facilitation of integrative processes." *Journal of Personality* 63: 397–427.

Ryan, R. M., and E. L. Deci. 2000. "Intrinsic and extrinsic motivations: Classic definitions and new directions." *Contemporary Educational Psychology* 25: 54–67.

Ryan, R. M., J. Kuhl, and E. L. Deci. 1997. "Nature and autonomy: Organizational view of social and neurobiological aspects of self-regulation in behavior and development." *Development and Psychopathology* 9: 701–728.

Sandage, S. J., and T. W. Wiens. 2001. "Contextualizing models of humility and forgiveness: A reply to Gassin." *Journal of Psychology and Theology* 29: 201.

Sendjaya, S., and J. Sarros. 2002. "Servant leadership: Its origins, development, and application in organizations." *Journal of Leadership Studies* 9, no. 2: 61.

Shirom, A. 2003. "Job-Related Burnout." In *Handbook of Occupational Health and Psychology,* edited by J. C. Quick and L. E. Tetrick. Washington, DC: American Psychological Association.

Sivanathan, N., and C. G. Fekken. 2002. "Emotional intelligence, moral reasoning and transformational leadership." *Leadership and Organization Development Journal* 23, no. 4: 198–204.

Spears, L. C. 2005. "The understanding and practice of servant leadership." *Proceedings of the Servant Leadership Research Roundtable.* http:// www.regent.edu/acad/global/publications/sl_proceedings/.

Spears, L. C. 2010. "Character and servant leadership: Ten characteristics of effective, caring leaders." *Journal of Virtues and Leadership* 1, no. 1: 25–30.

Spencer, L. J. 2007. "The new frontier of servant leadership." *Proceedings of the Servant Leadership Research Roundtable.* http://www.regent.edu/acad/global/publications/sl_proceedings/.

Stafford, M. C. 2010. *The Full Range Leadership Model: A Brief Primer.* Air University.

Stefano, S. F., and K. M. Wasylyshyn. 2005. "Integrity, courage, empathy (ICE): three leadership essentials." *Human Resource Planning* 28, no. 4: 5–7.

Stone, G. A., R. F. Russell, and K. Patterson. 2004. "Transformational versus servant leadership: A difference in leader focus." *Leadership and Organization Development Journal* 25, no. 4: 349–361.

Sutton, R. I. 2007. *The No Asshole Rule: Building a Civilized Workplace and Surviving One That Isn't.* New York: Warner Business Books.

Tan, C. 2010. "Everyday Compassion at Google." November. https://www.ted.com/talks/chade_meng_tan_everyday_compassion_at_google.

The Holy Bible (New International Version). 1984. Grand Rapids, MI: Zondervan Publishing House.

Thompson, B. L. 1995. Chapter 6, "Influencing Skills." In *The Manager's Handbook.* Richard D. Irwin, Inc.

Thoreau, H., and J. Levin. 2005. *Walden and Civil Disobedience.* New York: Barnes and Noble Classics.

Tracey, B. J., and T. R. Hinkin. 1998. "Transformational leadership or effective managerial practices?" *Group Organization Management* 23, no. 3 (September): 220–236.

Treasurer, B. 2014. "Getting Real about Leadership." [Blog]. University of California, San Diego. September 9. http://rady.ucsd.edu/blog/posts/getting-real-about-leadership.html.

Tucker, B. A., and R. F. Russell. 2004. "The influence of the transformational leader." *Journal of Leadership and Organizational Studies* 10, no. 4 (Spring): 103–111.

Tuckman, B. W. 1965. "Developmental sequence in small groups." *Psychological Bulletin* 63: 384–399.

Tuckman, B. W., and M. A. C. Jensen. 1977. "Stages of small group development revisited." *Group and Organizational Studies* 2: 419–427.

Tzu, L. 1996. *Tao Te Ching of Lao Tzu.* New York: St. Martin's Press.

Tzu, S. 1971. *The Art of War.* Translated by Samuel B. Griffith. New York, NY: Oxford University Press.

Ury, W. 1991. *Getting Past No: Negotiating with Difficult People.* New York: Bantam Books.

Vadell, J., and C. Ewing. 2011. "Intrinsic Motivation and servant leadership: A case for autonomy supporting work environments in the military." *International Journal of Humanities and Social Science* 1, no. 19: 249–251.

Vanderkam, L. 2012. *What the Most Successful People Do before Breakfast: A Short Guide to Making over Your Mornings—And Life.* Rego Park: Gildan Media Corp.

van Knippenberg, B., and D. van Knippenberg. 2005. "Leader Self-Sacrifice and Leadership Effectiveness: The Moderating Role of Leader Prototypicality." *Journal of Applied Psychology* 90, no. 1: 25–37. doi:10.1037/0021-9010.90.1.25.

Vergote, A. 1988. "A psychological approach to humility in the rule of St. Benedict." *American Benedictine Review* 39, no. 4: 404–429.

Vygotsky, L. S. 1978. *Mind in Society.* Cambridge, MA: Harvard University Press.

Wachowski, A., and L. Wachowski. 1999. *The Matrix.* Burbank, CA: Warner Bros. Pictures. DVD.

Wang, X., and J. M. Howell. 2010. "Exploring the dual-level effects of transformational leadership on followers." *Journal of Applied Psychology* 95, no. 6: 1134–1144. doi:10.1037/a0020754.

Ward, D., Lt Col. 2011. "Don't come to the dark side." *Defense AT&L, Better Buying Power,* special issue (September): 67–70.

Winston, B. E. 2003. "Extending Patterson's servant leadership model: Explaining how leaders and followers interact in a circular model." *Servant Leadership Roundtable.* Virginia Beach: Regent University.

Wood, D., J. Bruner, and G. Ross. 1976. "The role of tutoring in problem solving." *Journal of Child Psychology and Psychiatry* 17: 89–100.

Wu, J. B., A. S. Tsui, and A. J. Kinicki. 2010. "Consequences of differentiated leadership in groups." *Academy of Management Journal* 53: 90–106.

Yerkes, R. M., and J. D. Dodson. 1908. "The relation of strength of stimulus to rapidity of habit-formation." *Journal of Comparative Neurological Psychology* 18: 459–482.

Yukl, G. 1999. "An evaluation of conceptual weaknesses in transformational and charismatic leadership theories." *Leadership Quarterly* 10: 285–305.

Zaccaro, S. J., A. L. Rittman, and M. A. Marks. 2001. "Team leadership." *Leadership Quarterly* 12: 451–483.

Zachary, L. J. 2005. "Raising the bar in a mentoring culture." *Training and Development* 59, no. 6.

Zaleznik, A. 1992. "Managers and leaders: Are they different?" *Harvard Business Review* 70: 126–135.

Zoglio, S. W. 1994. *The Participative Leader.* Burr Ridge, IL: Irwin.

ADDITIONAL REFERENCES AND RECOMMENDED READING

Not all readers are leaders, but all leaders are readers.
—Harry Truman

Bass, B. M. 1985. *Leadership and Performance beyond Expectations*. New York: Free Press.

Bass, B. M., and B. J. Avolio. 1994. *Improving Organizational Effectiveness through Transformational Leadership*. Los Angeles: Sage Publications.

Blanchard, K., and S. Johnson. 1982. *The One Minute Manager*. New York, NY: Berkley Publishing Group.

Bryant, A., and A. L. Kazan. 2013. *Self-leadership: How to Become a More Successful, Efficient, and Effective Leader from the Inside Out*. New York: McGraw-Hill.

Bstan-'dzin-rgya-mtsho, Dalai Lama XIV. 2011. *Beyond Religion: Ethics for a Whole World*. Boston: Houghton Mifflin Harcourt.

Burkeman, O. 2012. *The Antidote: Happiness for People Who Can't Stand Positive Thinking*. Melbourne, Vic.: Text.

Burns, J. M. 1978. *Leadership*. New York: Harper and Row.

Cain, S. 2012. *Quiet: The Power of Introverts in a World That Can't Stop Talking*. New York: Crown Publishers.

Carnegie, D. 1998. *How to Win Friends and Influence People*. USA: Gallery.

Cashman, K. 2008. *Leadership from the Inside Out: Becoming a Leader for Life*. 2nd edition, revised and expanded. San Francisco: Berrett-Koehler Publishers.

Collins, J. 2001a. *Good to Great: Why Some Companies Make the Leap and Others Don't.* New York: Harper Business.

Covey, S. R. 1989. *The Seven Habits of Highly Effective People: Restoring the Character Ethic.* New York: Simon and Schuster.

De Pree, M. 1989. *Leadership Is an Art.* New York: Doubleday.

Frankl, V. E. 1963. *Man's Search for Meaning: An Introduction to Logotherapy.* New York: Pocket Books.

George, B. 2003. *Authentic Leadership: Rediscovering the Secrets to Creating Lasting Value.* San Francisco, CA: Jossey-Bass.

George, B. 2015. *Discover Your True North.* Hoboken, New Jersey: Wiley.

Goleman, D. 1995. *Emotional Intelligence: Why It Can Matter More Than IQ.* New York: Bantam Books.

Goleman, D. 2006. *Social Intelligence: The New Science of Human Relationships.* Bantam Books.

Greenleaf, R. K. 1977. *Servant Leadership.* Mahwah, NJ: Paulist Press.

Kouzes, J. M., and B. Z. Posner. 1993. *Credibility: How Leaders Gain and Lose It, Why People Demand It.* San Francisco: Jossey-Bass.

Manson, M. 2016. *The Subtle Art of Not Giving a F*ck: A Counterintuitive Approach to Living a Good Life.* New York: HarperOne.

Maxwell, J. 2014. *15 Invaluable Laws of Growth: Live Them and Reach Your Potential.* New York: Center Street.

Northouse, P. 2004. *Leadership: Theory and Practice.* Thousand Oaks, CA: Sage.

Pink, D. H. 2012. *Drive: The Surprising Truth about What Motivates Us.* New York: Riverhead Books.

Scott, K. M. 2017. *Radical Candor: How to Be a Kickass Boss without Losing Your Humanity.* 1st edition. New York: St. Martin's Press.

Sinek, S. 2011. *Start with Why: How Great Leaders Inspire Everyone to Take Action.* Portfolio/Penguin.

Taylor, L. 2013. *Tame Your Terrible Office Tyrant: How to Manage Childish Boss Behavior and Thrive in Your Job.* Hoboken, NJ: Wiley.

Welch, A., and S. Welch. 2005. *Winning.* HarperCollins.

ABOUT THE AUTHOR

Chris Ewing is a leadership consultant and educator working in health care administration, management consulting, and higher education. He formerly served as an Air Force officer, specializing in space and missile operations, and is the president of Perficitis Consulting Group, LLC, and the chief operating officer of Paradigm Leaders, LLC, both of which specialize in leadership development and management curriculum. He is also a director at Kaiser Permanente and the director of the Master of Science in Human Resource Management program and an associate professor at Touro University Worldwide. He has earned numerous degrees and certificates.

Made in the USA
Las Vegas, NV
28 January 2022

42451795R00118